Good Women
of a
Well-Blessed Land

Good Women
of a
Well-Blessed Land

WOMEN'S LIVES *in* COLONIAL AMERICA

Brandon Marie Miller

LERNER PUBLICATIONS COMPANY · MINNEAPOLIS

For two women who encouraged my love of history: Martha Luke Carr, my aunt, and in loving memory of my grandmother, Marie Smith Luke

My thanks to editor Sara Saetre for her expert fine-tuning, pushing, and prodding. I must also thank my husband, who often shared his lunchtime with last-minute trips to the Public Library of Cincinnati and Hamilton County, rechecking page numbers and quotes, and lugging home more books!

A Word about Language
English spelling, grammar, and punctuation have changed over the centuries. In quoted material, this book preserves all original spellings.

Lerner Publications Company
A division of Lerner Publishing Group
241 First Avenue North
Minneapolis, MN 55401 U.S.A.

Website address: www.lernerbooks.com

Library of Congress Cataloging-in-Publication Data

Miller, Brandon Marie.
    Good women of a well-blessed land : women's lives in colonial America / by Brandon Marie Miller.
        p.   cm. — (People's history)
    Summary: A social history of the American colonial period with a focus on the daily lives of women, including European immigrants, Native Americans, and slaves.
    Includes bibliographical references and index.
        ISBN: 0–8225–0032–9 (lib. bdg. : alk. paper)
        1. Women—United States—History—17th century—Juvenile literature. 2. Women—United States—History—18th century—Juvenile literature. 3. United States—Social life and customs—To 1775—Juvenile literature. [1. Women—United States—History—17th century. 2. Women—United States—History—18th century. 3. United States—Social life and customs—To 1775.] I. Title. II. Series.
HQ1416.M55 2003
305.4'0973'09032—dc21   2002008902

Manufactured in the United States of America
1 2 3 4 5 6 – JR – 08 07 06 05 04 03

Contents

In 1761 Phillis Wheatley was kidnapped and sold into slavery at age seven. She overcame the bonds of slavery and social prejudice to become America's first significant black writer.

AUTHOR'S NOTE

Hello! I'll admit here at the beginning: There is not enough room on these pages to include everything I'd like to tell about colonial America. Instead, this book focuses on women's lives—white women, black women, and Native American women—in the thirteen English colonies that later became the United States. Too often women's history has been neglected, labeled as less important. But I believe that examining the details of women's lives, and their place in the colonial world, can only deepen our understanding of the seventeenth and eighteenth centuries.

White women of the colonial era rarely put quill pen to paper to write journals and letters. Snooping historians, hundreds of years later, have few documents written by these women to shed light on their lives and thoughts. Studying Native American women and black women living in slavery is even harder. Personal stories written by them are nonexistent.

Even so, historians and archaeologists know quite a bit about women in colonial America. Archaeologists sift centuries of earth to uncover objects used by women. Historians sift through written records left by European men to find references to women. Other helpful documents include ship passenger lists, colonial newspapers, period books, court records, wills, and inventories taken after a husband's death. Artifacts such as paintings, clothing, and even tombstones provide clues about the lives of seventeenth- and eighteenth-century women.

Part of my curiosity about women in colonial America is personal. One twig of my family tree set roots in seventeenth-century Virginia. Virginia court records show that one of my ancestors, newly widowed Cecily Jordan, accepted a marriage proposal. She later refused to marry the man, choosing a different suitor instead. Cecily's change of heart was recorded when she was sued in the colony's first breach of promise case.

—*Brandon Marie Miller*

THE NATURAL INHABITANTS

*We were entertained with all love,
and kindness, and with as much
bounty . . . as they could possibly
devise.*
  —Englishman Arthur Barlowe,
   . writing of his welcome
  by Native Americans, 1584

The sun was just slipping below the treetops when word spread that a rowboat ferrying two white men was approaching the Roanoke village. As the wife of the chief's brother, one woman hastened to the water's edge to greet the sailors. Quickly, she gave orders to drag the strangers' boat onto the sand. Other helpers carried the strangers ashore on their backs. Then the woman escorted the guests to her home, a five-room lodge built from sweet smelling cedar.

Inside, she offered her guests a seat by the fire. She had her servants dry the strangers' wet clothes and bathe their feet in warmed water. Dish after dish of food was presented for the strangers' pleasure: venison stew, boiled fish, juicy melons, wine, and water flavored with sassafras, ginger, and black cinnamon.

Suddenly several native men returned from hunting and entered the house carrying bows and arrows. The woman spied the fear freezing the strangers' faces and asked the hunters to put their weapons outside. At the evening's end, her guests rowed back to their ship laden with pots of food and invitations to return.

The two lucky guests were English sea captains whose voyage of exploration to America had been sponsored by Sir Walter Raleigh. In the written report of their visit to present-day North Carolina, the gracious Native American woman is referred to only as "the wife of Granganimo the king's brother." But the Englishmen praised her beauty, admired her coral and pearl jewelry, and commented on the fine copper earrings of her many servants. The Englishmen also praised the villagers, "for a more kinde and loving people there can not be found in the worlde."

Like many Native American women before and after her, Granganimo's wife greeted the Europeans with generosity and assistance. And like many Native American women before and after her, the reward she received for her hospitality was one of pain. Not many years later, her village was burned, destroyed by the first English colonists at Roanoke.

HOUSEHOLD AFFAIRS

In 1600 an estimated 400,000 Native Americans farmed and hunted east of the Appalachian Mountains along a coastline stretching from Canada to Florida. The native inhabitants of these vast lands were diverse peoples, speaking different languages, living under different social orders, and practicing different religions.

Most Native Americans lived in villages. Some villages were nothing more than a few houses. Others were large communities of fifty lodges or more surrounded by a stockade of logs sharpened like spears. Within the larger group of the tribe, people often banded together by family ties, known as clans. Villagers hiked a network of trails through towering forests. They canoed rivers far and wide to trade and create alliances among tribes.

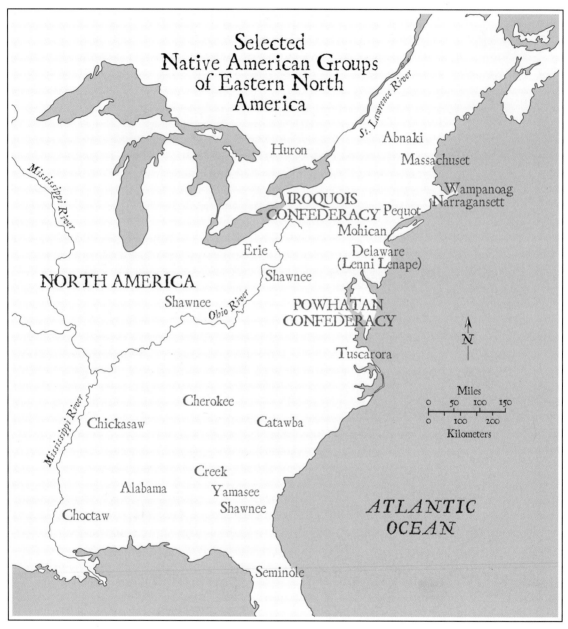

Native American peoples of eastern North America had established thriving societies long before the arrival of the first European settlers.

Men were often away from the village, engaged in war, diplomacy, and trade. They hunted animals and birds in the woods and fished in the ocean and streams. After a winter spent tracking game over miles of rough ground, men opted for lighter work in summer. They mended snowshoes, repaired canoes, crafted new weapons, and kept in shape playing sports.

A woman's life centered on her village and home. Without her efforts, the tribe could not survive. "In the management of household affairs the husband leaves everything to his wife and never interferes," explained a missionary (European religious teacher) who lived among the Lenni Lenape (the Delaware).

A woman fetched water and gathered wood to stoke her cooking fires and warm her home. She created the tools and goods her family needed: woven baskets and sacks, clay pots, leather pouches, and dishes made of tree bark.

Women also built the tribes' homes. In some tribes, such as the Wampanoag, Narragansett, and Powhatan, women created houses by layering tightly woven mats over an arching frame of bent poles. Women fashioned the mats from dried winter grasses or dried cattails, often weaving designs into their work. In the late 1630s, English colonist Roger Williams wrote that Narragansett homes were "embroydered" so beautifully that the designs made "as fair a show as Hangings [tapestries] with us." Mat-covered houses usually had one room about sixteen feet long by fourteen feet wide. A smoke hole in the roof, covered with a flap, let smoke drift up and out. In hot weather, the sides of the house rolled up to receive cool breezes. The homes were also portable. A woman could pack and move poles and mats as needed, closer to winter hunting grounds or summer fields.

Women in other tribes used other construction methods. Iroquois women covered their longhouses with bark. Some of these homes measured fifty to one hundred feet long and housed as many as twenty families. Women in southern tribes, such as the Cherokee and the Choctaw, covered a rectangular pole frame with a mixture of

The Native American village of Pomelock stood on Roanoke Island. Palisades (defensive fencing) protected the village of mat houses and its inhabitants.

packed clay and crushed shells, bark, or grasses. Thatched roofs kept these houses snug.

"SHE COOKS VICTUALS REGULARLY"

Men provided meat and fish, but women provided all other foods. Unlike farming in Europe, which was mostly left to men, farmwork in Native American villages was a female task. Just after dawn, women headed to the fields with small children in tow. They worked together, singing and chatting, digging and hoeing with clamshells and deer-bone tools. Older women protected the crops from animals. One European settler observed women scolding wayward horses away from tender plants and fretting "at the very shadow of a crow."

The main staples of Native American diets were corn, beans, and squash (called the Three Sisters by the Iroquois). Women planted several kinds of corn. James Adair, a trader in the Carolinas among the Cherokee, Catawba, and other tribes, described yellow "hommony corn;" "small corn," which ripened quickly; and a large white corn called bread corn.

Women preserved a quantity of food, including corn, for winter meals. Dried corn was stashed in large pots buried in the ground. Women also cut thin slices of pumpkin, fish, and meat, then dried the strips on racks in the sun or over a smoky fire.

Native American women were often the keepers of village horticulture. They selected, planted, and harvested the best food crops, including maize, or corn, **right.**

Grinding corn between stones was a frequent chore. Women patted a cornmeal-and-water mixture into flat cakes that baked nestled in hot ashes. They simmered mixtures of meat, roots, and vegetables over a fire. They roasted hunks of fresh meat until its dripping fat hissed into the flames.

To supplement crops, Native American women picked wild fruits such as strawberries and cranberries. They dug edible roots in the forest, gathered baskets of nuts, and harvested clams along the seashore. In late winter, they collected sap from maple trees and boiled it into sweet syrup.

A Native American woman grinds corn into cornmeal. Native American women used cornmeal in a variety of dishes.

In many American Indian cultures of eastern North America, women were
responsible for village food supplies. Male hunters turned over the game
they killed to their wives, sisters, and mothers.

Women controlled how and when food was doled out. A man gave
up his control over meat, once home from hunting. The woman
"may then do what she pleases with it," one missionary marveled.
"[Her husband] says nothing, if she even gives the greatest part of it
to her friends, which is a very common custom." If women wished to
stop their men from going to war, they withheld the dried corn and
dried meat necessary to feed the war party.

Women were generous with their food supplies. A woman who
provided for others "when meat has been secured" earned the respect
of her people.

CLOTHES ON OUR BACKS

Animals provided hides for clothing as well as meat. Women tanned the
hides into a supple, yellowish leather. First they soaked the hides in water
and scraped off the hair. They resoaked the hides in a chemical mixture of
crushed deer brains and water. The skin was then stretched on a rack.

An Iroquois woman and child dressed in traditional clothing, about 1650. Native American women created many kinds of clothing suitable for different climates, purposes, and occasions.

The women rubbed the stretched leather over and over with a stone or dull hatchet to force out water and grease. Once rubbed and dried, the softened leather could be sliced with a knife and sewed into clothes with a bone needle and deer sinews. For winter warmth, Native American women fashioned thick fur robes and blankets.

Dresses, skirts, shirts, leggings, and moccasins made from tanned skins felt buttery soft. But the sturdy garments easily withstood snags from branches and brambles. A woman expressed her creative side by decorating clothes and other objects with shells, bone beads, dyed porcupine quills, and paints. People seldom washed their clothes because washing would destroy the garments. Native Americans often wore clothing until the garments literally fell apart.

"DOING JUST WHAT THEY LIKE"

Native American women labored hard at jobs that were often physically demanding. Yet they were free to set their own work pace, and they usually shared chores. They also saved time for fun. In the 1630s, French missionary Gabriel Sagard complained that native women found "plenty of time to waste." Women enjoyed themselves "in gaming, going to dances and feasts, chatting and killing time," he wrote. Even worse, in his opinion, they were used to "doing just what they like with their leisure."

Many Native Americans kept house with a single spouse. In some tribes, however, a husband lived with more than one wife. A man might be expected to marry his brother's widow, as a way of providing care for her. Some tribes believed a man should marry all the sisters in one family. The first (or eldest) wife usually held an honored status. Additional wives served as extra workers.

A would-be husband wooed his sweetheart—and her family—with gifts. When he wanted to marry, he sought permission from the bride's parents or from an older female relative. Often the man needed to prove his worth. Could he provide meat and protection for his new wife? Some tribes put the groom through a yearlong test, observing him and his intended as the two lived with her family. In tribes of the Iroquois confederacy—the Cayuga, Mohawk, Oneida, Onondaga, and Seneca—the husband joined his new wife's clan.

Either partner was free to end an unhappy union. The choice of walking away gave Native American women an independence not shared by white women. Yet the ease of dissolving a marriage did not make divorce common. "I know many couples," reported European colonist Roger Williams, "that have lived twenty, thirty, forty yeares together." Rarely did one spouse put the other aside if they had children, who remained in the care of the mother and her clan. "The mother's title rests on the law of nature," noted a French observer in the 1690s, "since no one can dispute that she is the mother of the children whom she has brought into the world."

MOTHERHOOD

Most native peoples believed pregnancy linked a woman to mysterious and dangerous forces of nature. "Pregnant women among them cause, they say, many misfortunes," reported Jesuit priest Francois du Peron, "for they cause the husband not to take anything in the hunt; if one of them enters a cabin where there is a sick person, he grows worse; if she looks at the animal that is being pursued, it can no longer be captured."

As labor began, most Native American women left their homes for a specially prepared hut. The mother gave birth with aid from a midwife or relative, or perhaps even alone. As a warrior tested his bravery in battle, so a woman displayed hers by not crying out with the pain of childbirth. To surrender to pain would shame her. Roger Williams was astounded to observe that native women "are scarcely heard to groane" during childbirth. Not realizing that native women were simply being brave, European males concluded that native women must be made differently than white women. "The [native] Women of America have very easy Travail [labor] with their children...," noted southern trader John Lawson. "Besides, they are unacquainted with those severe Pains which follow the Birth in our European Women."

Native American mothers toted their babies upright in snug wooden cradleboards fashioned by the fathers. The mother decorated her child's cradleboard with paint, beads, and feathers. Carrying the baby on her back freed her arms for work. She could also prop the cradleboard against a tree trunk or hang it from a branch. Instead of using diapers, mothers stuffed moss or fluff from river cattails inside the cradleboard around their babies.

Mothers started early to teach their children to endure discomfort. They dowsed infants in cold water or snow. They allowed toddlers outside without clothes. Seasoning children to hardship meant teaching them survival. Mothers also trained their daughters in the ways of women's work. Turning work into play, mothers had little girls pound corn, gather sticks, and pull weeds.

Native American mothers rarely struck their children. Many Europeans found this neglect of punishment shocking. If a Native American mother wanted to scold her daughter, she might simply burst into tears and say, "Thou dishonourest me." Jesuit priest Pierre de

Native American mothers used cradleboards, **far right,** *and slings,* **right,** *to safely hold their babies. (To see another example of a cradleboard, turn back to page 14.)*

Charlevoix declared, "It seldom happens that this sort of reproof [scolding] fails." The greatest punishment he witnessed was a mother flicking water in her child's face. "It would seem . . . that a childhood so ill instructed, should be followed by a very . . . turbulent state of youth," he wrote, "[but] the Indians are naturally quiet and . . . masters of themselves." Native American mothers set that example for their children from birth.

IN THIS NEW DISCOVERED VIRGINIA

In a newe plantation it is not knowen whether man or woman be the most necessary.
—Virginia House of Burgesses, an elected legislature, July 1619

In May 1607, 110 Englishmen established a foothold at "James Towne," Virginia. Their chosen site was along a wide river that flowed into the Chesapeake Bay. King James I had granted the tiny, new colony vast lands—stretching for unknown miles west as far as the Pacific Ocean.

Less than a year and a half later, Captain John Smith of the colony recorded: "The first gentlewoman and woman-servant . . . arrived." The new arrivals were Anne Forrest, wife of a colonist, and her unmarried maid, Anne Burras. As a young, single woman, Anne Burras was a rare prize. Within months she married John Laydon in the colony's first wedding.

The condition of their new hometown most likely shocked the two women. Crowded huts with dirt floors served as houses. The women had seldom experienced such heat and humidity in England. And the land, though beautiful, seemed uncontrollably wild and infested with insects and vermin.

In August 1609, Jamestown welcomed a new wave of colonists, including some women and children. Jamestown's population swelled to five hundred. None of the colonists imagined the desperate hardships they were about to face.

"THE WANT OF WOMEN"

As early as 1609, broadsides (posters) nailed up in England had encouraged single women to emigrate to Jamestown "for the better strengthening of the colony." Virginia offered husbands, a home, and a new life—with a touch of adventure.

While some women answered the New World's call, others were sent against their will. Kidnappers grabbed some women off English streets and sold them in Virginia as servants. One song lilting through London's taverns told the tale of "The Woman Outwitted: or the Weaver's Wife cunningly catch'd in a Trap, by her Husband, who sold her for ten Pounds, and sent her to Virginny."

In 1619 the Virginia Company (a group of London investors seeking to profit from the resources of the New World) actively enlisted "wives for Virginia." The investors realized that a shipload of females would "tye and roote the Planters myndes [minds] to Virginia by the bonds of wives and children." About ninety women arrived in Virginia in February and March of 1620.

In 1621 the company began a new campaign for "younge, handsome, and honestlie educated Maides." Young women hoping to be chosen supplied recommendations laced with words such as *honest, sober,* and *industrious.* Most listed skills that included brewing, baking, and sewing.

The company selected fifty-seven women "specially recommended for their good bringing up." The women ranged in age from fifteen to

Enticed by promises of marriage, prosperity, and adventure, women colonists arrive at the Jamestown settlement in 1621.

twenty-six. Most of them, like Martha Baker, were around twenty years old. Three of them, such as Elizabeth Grinbey, age twenty-six, were widows. Twenty women were teenagers. Jane Dier, for example, was about fifteen or sixteen. Eleven of the women, including Lucy Remnant, had no living parents. Eleven others, like Elizabeth Neville, had lost their fathers.

What courage or desperation drove a young woman to make the dangerous voyage across the Atlantic to an uncertain future? One incentive was her chance to meet the "honest and industrious Planters" there. The planters would reimburse the Virginia Company for the cost of bringing their future brides to Virginia. The price was 150 pounds of Virginia's new currency—tobacco.

The company supplied each woman with petticoats, caps, an apron, two pairs of shoes, and six pairs of sheets. Within months of their arrival in the autumn of 1621, many of the women were, indeed, married.

DARK DAYS

Women must have wondered what was expected of them in this "new world." At home in England, a woman could buy bread—or at least a sack of flour—from a miller in the village. At home, she could grow vegetables and herbs in a patch of kitchen garden. She could keep a cow or a few goats to milk, so she could make cheese and churn butter. She could buy cloth to sew clothes for her family. But in Jamestown, she found these simple acts difficult or impossible.

Society itself was missing. Where were all the farmers, the laborers, the servants? Where were the craftsmen, tradespeople, and merchants with their wares? Where were the churchmen and the great stone cathedrals? Where were the lords and ladies, clad in their laces and velvet?

The crude, often lonely, conditions of early settlements such as Jamestown, **above,** *were alien to what the first women colonists had known in England.*

Most of all, where were the women? For everywhere a Jamestown woman looked, she saw six men for every female face. There were other female faces in Virginia, of course, but Englishwomen did not consider Native American women their equals. The Jamestown colonists often huddled behind their stockade walls, fearful to venture into dark woods filled with "skulking savages."

English people had little experience hunting game or searching for edible plants. There might be fish in the sea, birds in the air, and "beasts" in the woods. But as colony leader John Smith wrote, "They are so wild and we so weake and ignorant, we cannot much trouble them [by hunting]."

Chopping down enough trees to create farm fields seemed overwhelming. In England most people didn't have to know how to wield an ax. They collected twigs and fallen branches for fuel. How could colonists possibly hack down a thick forest to clear a field "penetrable For the Plough?" wondered one colony backer.

Most Jamestown colonists were considered "gentlemen" and had never plowed or planted. Many believed "rooting in the ground" was beneath their dignity—even if it meant growing crops to feed themselves. They'd signed on for adventure and profit, expecting a quick return to a comfortable life in England. Unable to raise enough crops, the colonists relied mostly on corn supplied by Native Americans and on the dwindling foodstuffs they'd brought on their ships.

The hot, humid climate also frightened people. They feared that heat sapped fluid from a person's blood. "Great Sweating," warned medical writer William Vaughan, left the "inner parts" cold and withered. Colonists sickened with what they called ague (probably malaria), suffering through waves of chills and fevers, nausea and vomiting.

Many people died from sickness and starvation. At one point, only sixty men, women, and children remained alive out of five hundred colonists. Survivors gnawed acorns, rats, snakes, roots, and sometimes a bit of fish. John Smith reported that one hungry man murdered "his wife as she slept . . . & fedd upon her till he had clean devoured all her parts saveinge [except] her head." The husband was executed, "burned for his horrible villany."

FIRST CONTACT BETWEEN TWO WORLDS

Jamestown lay in an area inhabited by Algonquin-speaking tribes. These tribes were unified under a powerful man the English called Powhatan. Even before the first colonists rowed ashore at Jamestown, people of the Powhatan Confederacy—as well as other Native Americans—had sampled European goods carried by traders and explorers who had visited the New World.

The strangers with their pale skin and many shades of hair aroused the curiosity of native people. European ships, so much larger than native canoes, seemed like floating islands on the sea. And the white people wore clothes in colors and fabrics amazing to behold. Sunlight flashed from their helmets and armor. The Europeans possessed wonders: iron hoes, mirrors, clocks, and books. Their copper kettles were so thin, yet unbreakable. The blades of their knives and hatchets gleamed sharper and stronger than anything the natives had. Most startling of all—and terrifying—was the fact that the newcomers carried guns that exploded in smoke and a noise louder than any crack of thunder.

Many tribes referred to whites by their remarkable goods, calling them "Coatmen," "Swordmen," "Iron-Workers," and "Clothmakers." From first contact, Native Americans were more than willing to trade food and information for the amazing gifts of the Europeans.

Contact with Europeans, however, meant contact with European diseases that native people had never encountered before, diseases such as smallpox, measles, diphtheria, and influenza. Europeans, who were regularly exposed to such illnesses, had built up some resistance to them. In contrast, Native Americans were devastated by them. Raging fevers, vomiting, diarrhea, and racking coughs spread from lodge to lodge, leaving no one well enough to fetch water, food, or wood. In some cases, entire villages of native people were wiped out.

Contact between the Powhatan and the English at Jamestown, such as at the trade meeting above, seesawed between peace and conflict. Tensions grew as the settlers demanded more Powhatan land and resources.

The European settlers viewed native culture and religion as inferior to their own. To their eyes, it seemed native men forced women to do all the work. Meanwhile, native men seemed to spend all their time hunting and fishing, which seemed like sporting fun to the English. The women's lives, wrote John Smith, "be very painful and the men often idle. The women and children do the rest of the work." Another colonist marveled, "It is almost incredible what burthens [burdens] the poore women carry of Corne, of Fish, of Beanes, of Mats, and a childe besides."

"THIS LADY POCAHONTAS"

The "most deare and wel-beloved daughter" of Chief Powhatan of the Powhatan Confederacy was a twelve-year-old girl called Pocahontas. From the start, Pocahontas visited Jamestown, learning some English and teaching words of her language to the strangers.

The relationship between the Powhatans and the colonists simmered with tension, however. Late in 1607, the Powhatans had captured John Smith and sentenced him to death. According to Smith, just as his head was about to be crushed between two stones, Pocahontas begged her father to spare the Englishman's life. Powhatan relented, and Smith returned safely to Jamestown.

Pocahontas continued serving as a peacemaker between Powhatan and the Europeans. In May 1608, she successfully pleaded for the release of several Native Americans imprisoned at Jamestown. Smith recorded that in early 1609, Pocahontas warned the settlement of a planned attack.

In 1613 Englishmen kidnapped Pocahontas, hoping to pressure Powhatan into releasing new English captives. The colonists also demanded bushels of Indian corn in exchange for the girl's return. Powhatan took his time replying. During the months Pocahontas spent as a hostage, she studied English and the Christian religion.

She also met a widower named John Rolfe. Rolfe had been the first to plant a popular West Indies tobacco in the colony. After he began shipping his harvests to Europe, demand for tobacco soared. Soon Virginians were clearing land (with a slash-and-burn method learned from Native Americans) and blanketing the fields with tobacco plants.

Rolfe began courting Pocahontas. But he struggled with his attraction for her. The young woman's "education hath been rude," he explained in a letter, "her manners barbarous, her generation accursed." Eventually Pocahontas converted to Christianity. She was christened with an English name—Rebecca. She married Rolfe at Jamestown in April 1614, in a ceremony attended by her brothers and uncle. For a time, the marriage brought peace between the colonists and Powhatan.

In June 1616, Pocahontas, her husband, and their baby son, Thomas, sailed for England. London's citizens entertained Pocahontas like visiting royalty, throwing balls and dinners in her honor. Even King James I met the intriguing young woman from Virginia.

The damp cold, the crowding, and the filth of London took its toll on Pocahontas, however. The family was already aboard ship,

Pocahontas in England, 1616, shortly before her death. Born Matoaka, she is best known for her courageous efforts to make peace between her people, the Powhatan, and the English settlers at Jamestown.

returning to Virginia, when she fell deadly ill in March 1617. Pocahontas was probably only twenty-two years old when her extraordinary life ended. Rolfe buried her in Gravesend, England. "She next under God," wrote Smith, "was . . . the instrument to preserve this colony from death, famine and utter confusion." Certainly her intelligence and curiosity had bridged two worlds.

GROWING VERY SLOWLY

Chief Powhatan died about a year after his daughter Pocahontas. With their deaths, hope for peace in Virginia died, too. Virginia's Native Americans had grown weary of years of strain, loss, and English arrogance. They had witnessed the destruction of forests, wild game, crops and fields, villages and homes. The Powhatan Confederacy was led at this time by Powhatan's half brother Opechancanough. In the early morning of March 22, 1622, Opechancanough's warriors struck back, attacking

Virginia's scattered James River settlements. Records show that 347 colonists died, including some of the women sent as "wives for Virginia."

Another group of people, small in numbers, were also experiencing Virginia's early struggles. The first African Americans had arrived from Africa or the West Indies (islands in the Caribbean Sea). Some came as slaves, but most came as indentured servants.

One woman known as "Mary, an African" arrived just months after the March 22, 1622, attack by the Powhatans. She worked as an indentured servant on a James River tobacco farm. Only five of the farm's fifty-five workers had survived the grim events of March 22. Out of those five, Mary found Antonio, an African man. Once their years as servants lay behind them, Mary and her husband took the names Mary and Anthony Johnson. They settled on a 250-acre farm.

Death hovered over Virginia's early years. Disease, lack of food, and clashes between settlers and their Native American neighbors ensured that Virginia's population grew slowly. By 1625, only 35 of the nearly 150 women who had immigrated to the colony remained alive.

Much of the development of the colonies would not have been possible without the labor of African American women and men. The first African Americans came to North America as indentured servants (people who agreed to work for someone else for a set number of years). Or, like the women and men at left, they came as slaves.

GOODWIVES TO NEW ENGLAND

A woman has been the breeder and nourisher of all these distempers.
—John Winthrop, governor of Massachusetts Bay Colony, writing about Anne Hutchinson, 1644

Five hundred miles north of Virginia, in December 1620, passengers on board the *Mayflower* glimpsed their new home. Eighteen women gathered along the ship's deck rail, facing that "hidious and desolate wilderness." What raced through their minds? Elizabeth Hopkins and Susannah White cradled infants in their arms, babies born during the voyage from England. Unlike the majority of women who traveled to Virginia—young and alone—the women of the *Mayflower* had dutifully followed husbands or fathers into the wilderness.

THE PILGRIMS OF PLYMOUTH

The settlers (called Pilgrims by later generations) established England's second colony at Plymouth in Massachusetts. About half of them were separatists. Separatists had belonged to the Church of England. They felt the church had slipped into corruption and so decided to "separate" from it. Many explored religious freedom in Holland for more than a decade before deciding to establish their own base in America. Because of the dangerous voyage and uncertain future, some parents had left small children behind with relatives in Europe. Many goodwives (a title given to married women) must have felt keen anguish, not knowing whether they would ever see their children again.

Those first weeks, women and children spent most of their time living on the *Mayflower*. Sometimes they rowed ashore to do laundry and to gather for church services. The men prepared crude shelters and made first contact with the Wampanoag tribe. When the Englishmen stumbled across an empty Native American village while scouting the area, they were not above robbing the villagers' homes. "Some of the best things we took away with us," recorded William Bradford, colony leader.

The Pilgrims of Plymouth arrived in December of 1620, facing a harsh New England winter without permanent shelter and with limited supplies.

***Pilgrims receiving Massasoit, chief of the Wampanoag. Early meetings
between the Pilgrims and Wampanoag were cautious but peaceful.***

Like the Jamestown settlers, the Plymouth colonists faced a horren-
dous beginning. Tragedy struck early. Mary Allerton gave birth to a
stillborn son. Dorothy Bradford fell overboard and drowned. Disease
claimed weakened colonists as easy victims. William Bradford wrote:

> Being the depth of winter, and wanting houses and other
> comforts; being infected with the scurvie and other dis-
> eases, which this long vioage [voyage] . . . had brought upon
> them . . . that of 100 and odd persons, scarce 50 remained.
> And of these in the time of most distres, ther was but 6 or
> 7 sound persons.

By April 1621, Susanna White, Mary Brewster, Elizabeth Hopkins,
and Eleanor Billington formed a tiny circle of the sole female survivors. Like Jamestown, Plymouth clung to life with aid from Native
Americans and with the arrival of ships with new supplies and
colonists. With the help of a few teenage girls like Priscila Mullins

and Desire Minter, the handful of Plymouth females cooked and washed clothes for all the colonists and provided care for children left motherless or orphaned.

Seemingly the women resented this communal work, however. Before long, every family was granted its own parcel of land. This resulted in "very good success." Bradford observed:

> The women now went willingly into the field, and took their little ones with them to set corn; which before . . . to have compelled [forced] would have been thought great tyranny and oppression. . . . For men's wives to be commanded to do service for other men, as dressing meat, washing their clothes, etc., they deemed it a kind of slavery, neither could many husbands well brook it.

THE PURITANS OF MASSACHUSETTS BAY

In March 1630, Margaret Winthrop bid farewell to her husband John. He was leaving their home in England to lead a wave of colonists bound for Massachusetts Bay. Margaret (whom John called "my sweet soule") would not see her husband again for a year and a half. Husband and wife promised that on "mundayes [Mondays] and frydayes [Fridays] at 5: of the clocke at night, we shall meet in spiritt till we meet in person."

The Winthrops were Puritans. Like the colonists at Plymouth, the Puritans had also broken with the Church of England. They even faced threats of imprisonment for criticizing the English government. In America, they hoped to create a pure church, a new spiritual community based on the Bible's teachings. Winthrop hoped their "city on a hill" would shine as a beacon for others to follow.

After seventy-eight days at sea, one thousand new settlers arrived in Massachusetts Bay. Although weak from scurvy and dysentery, they set to work immediately. They began establishing towns circling Boston Harbor. They traded with Native Americans for corn and fish. Eighty people decided that the harsh life of a colonist was not for them. They sailed with the ship *Arabella* when it returned to England to fetch emergency supplies.

For Puritans like John Winthrop, however, each hardship arrived as a test from God. A faithful Puritan strove to do well on each test. The very founding of Massachusetts Bay Colony was meant to serve God. In November 1631, Margaret finally joined John Winthrop in the colony, along with their eight children.

During the 1630s and 1640s, thousands of Puritans fled England for Massachusetts Bay Colony. The area—known even then as New England—expanded into a land of settled towns, small farms, and frontier outposts. Yet the process of uprooting, of leaving family and community in England, remained difficult.

Eighteen-year-old Anne Bradstreet (1612–1672) migrated with her family and husband in 1630. Upon her arrival in Massachusetts, her "heart rose" with unhappiness. Bradstreet grew depressed and ill. Only when she accepted that her new life "was the way of God" could she start again and "join the church at Boston."

A MOST HORRIBLE LAMENTATION

Many Puritans also viewed conflict with Native Americans as a test of the Puritan experiment. From 1636 to 1637, the Puritans waged war on the Pequot tribe in Connecticut. Many Pequot were killed. Still more were taken by force to the West Indies in the Caribbean, where they were sold into slavery. The Puritans hailed their victory as a triumph for God's chosen people.

Years later, Puritans fought Metacom, the Wampanoag leader also known as King Philip, in a conflict that spread across New England. Joining Metacom in his fight to save their homelands was a Wampanoag woman, Weetamoo. She led three hundred warriors against the English. Colonists had killed Weetamoo's first and second husband. Her child and sister had been captured by the English and sold as slaves. Mary Rowlandson, a white woman captured during the war, had no sense of Weetamoo's tragedies, describing her only as a "severe and proud Dame."

Wampanoag leader Metacom, who died at the hands of the English settlers, is shown at right. Misunderstanding, prejudice, and greed led English settlers to believe they had a right to rid the colonies of Native Americans.

When Metacom and Weetamoo were killed, Puritan officials rejoiced. They followed a centuries-old custom and displayed the heads of the Native American leaders on spiked poles. "The Indians who were prisoners there, knew it presently," wrote Increase Mather, a minister, "and made a most horrible and diabolical Lamentation, crying out that it was their Queens head."

IN GOD'S GRACE

Politics and social life were tied to religion in Massachusetts Bay Colony. Political power rested with those men who owned property and were selected as full members into the Puritan church. When Puritans gathered for worship, the congregation sat according to their wealth, sex, and even age.

Puritans believed women, like men, could receive God's grace and attain membership in the church. But women were treated differently from men. During day-long services, they crammed onto church benches with their children—separated from male worshippers.

No women were ministers. No women held church office. No women signed church covenants. No women had a public voice in selecting new ministers. And certainly no women preached.

Women who were nursing babies and raising a house full of young ones had a hard time walking miles into town to attend church. In winter, many women could not attend church at all. John Winthrop described the ordeal of Mrs. Dalkin, who nearly drowned crossing a swollen river on her way to church. Her husband could not swim, but luckily the family dog plunged into the water. "She caught hold on the dog's tail, so he drew her to shore and saved her life," Winthrop noted in his journal.

Although officially powerless, New England women wielded some influence behind the scenes. A few well-placed words from women could ruin a minister's reputation. When Jeremiah Shepard lost his

Led by a minister and protected by guards, Pilgrim mothers and daughters walk to church.

position, he blamed Goodwife Elithorp, claiming she hated him. "If she had an opportunity he doubted not but she would cut his throat," recorded retired minister Samuel Phillips. Shepard also faced opposition from Phillips's wife. The steely matron quietly spread the word that young Shepard seriously neglected his studies.

Women's voices were often heard through their husbands, who pushed church elders to set up new churches in outlying areas. One outlying parish wrangled with the town of Ipswich over a new church and minister. A local church history related the event:

> While we were in this great conflict . . . som women without the knowledge of theire husbands, and with the advice of some few men went to other towns and got help and raised the house that we intended for a meeting house [church] if we could git liberty.

For their part in establishing a new church, three wives were charged with contempt of authority.

"ONE MISTRIS HUTCHINSON"

Anne Hutchinson (1591–1643), her husband, and their twelve children followed their minister to Massachusetts Bay Colony in 1634. Anne's father, a clergyman, had encouraged his intelligent daughter's discussions of religion. In Boston, Anne led a small prayer group for women. Attendance at their weekly meetings eventually mushroomed into crowds of people—over sixty men and women—who packed the Hutchinson house. Women were not supposed to teach religion. "We do no more," Anne explained, "but read the notes of our teachers Sermons, and then reason of them by searching the Scriptures."

Puritan leaders, however, viewed the situation as explosive. It was daring to question ministers' interpretations of scripture. The fact that Anne was a woman made the situation even worse. John Winthrop described Anne as "haughty and fierce . . . more bold than a man." Her lack of humility and shame angered him and other Puritan authorities.

Anne Hutchinson appears before the leaders of the Massachusetts Bay Colony in 1638. Outspoken and strong, she was banished from the colony for challenging Puritan leaders.

Anne challenged the very structure of colonial society, which believed women were beneath men. Her aim, claimed Winthrop, was "the utter subversion both of Churches and civill state."

Eventually Anne was tried by a civil court and a church court. One judge claimed that Anne had belittled "the honour and authority of the publick Ministry." She had acted as if the minister "could not deliver his matter so clearly to the hearers" as Anne could herself.

Both courts condemned Anne. She was excommunicated from the church (denied church membership) and banished from the colony in 1638. Anne and her family journeyed to Rhode Island, a colony founded in 1636 by Roger Williams, another Puritan exiled from Massachusetts. In 1643, after moving to the Dutch colony of New Amsterdam (later New York), Anne Hutchinson was killed at her farm during a Native American raid.

After the Hutchinson case, Puritan authorities cracked down even harder on religious dissenters. Sarah Keayne was punished for preaching in a "mixed assembly" of men and women. Her husband claimed she had "unwifed herself."

The Quakers, another religious group, disregarded the need for ministers altogether. They believed each person possessed an "inner light" that communicated directly with God. In 1658 one follower of Anne Hutchinson, Mary Dyer, returned to Boston as a Quaker. Puritan authorities viewed Quakers as heretics, troublemakers opposed to the views of the Puritan church. They ordered Dyer be hanged on Boston Common in 1660. Other Massachusetts officials tied three Quaker women to the back of a cart and whipped them as they staggered in a procession winding from town to town.

"A VIRTUOUS WOMAN"

"Families . . . are the first foundation of Humane Societies. . . ," wrote Samuel Willard in *A Compleat Body of Divinity,* "and do . . . require there be Order in them, without which Mankind would fall." Within all colonial families, the husband was seen as master over all. His wife was beneath him, yet above her children and servants.

A sterling compliment for a colonial woman was the title "notable housewife." A wife might temporarily transform into a "deputy husband" if her mate was ill or away and men's work needed to be done. But she served first as a housewife who "worketh willingly with her hands" and "eateth not the bread of idleness."

The model for a perfect woman appeared in Proverbs 31. "Who can find a virtuous woman?" the proverb asked, "For her price is far above rubies." A virtuous woman proved a good neighbor and "stretcheth out her hand to the poor." She ruled as a good mistress, stern but kind, to her servants. She dressed with modesty, for "strength and honour are her clothing." And at heaven's gate, ended the proverb, "Let her own works praise her."

WEARY, WEARY, WEARY, O

Their servants they distinguish by the names of slaves for life, and servants for a time.

—Robert Beverly, on the difference between a "slave" and a "servant," 1705

New colonies took hold throughout the 1600s. New Hampshire, Connecticut, and Rhode Island joined Massachusetts in New England. Maryland became Virginia's neighbor in the lands surrounding the Chesapeake Bay. New York, New Jersey, Pennsylvania, and Delaware came to be called the middle colonies.

Realizing women were vital to a colony's success, each new colony advertised abroad for single females. And what a rosy picture the advertisements painted! In the 1634 pamphlet *New England's Prospect,* the author guaranteed that an Englishwoman's life in the New World would be one of ease and "happinesse."

Since a woman's main duty in the New World was to marry and raise children, her hope of finding a husband was a strong lure to emigrate there. After all, the colonies had many more men than women.

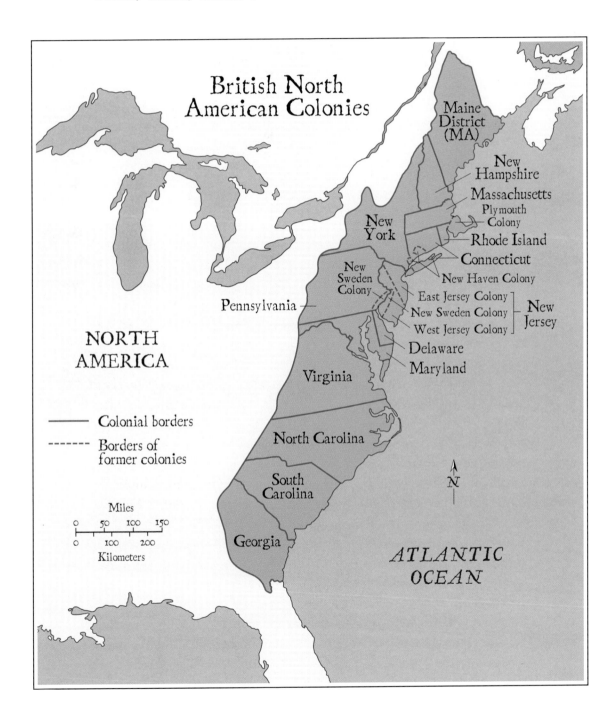

British North
American Colonies

Maine
District
(MA)

New
Hampshire

Massachusetts

Plymouth
Colony

New
York

Rhode Island

Connecticut

New Haven Colony

New
Sweden
Colony

East Jersey Colony

New Sweden Colony

New
Jersey

West Jersey Colony

Pennsylvania

Delaware

Maryland

NORTH
AMERICA

Virginia

—————— Colonial borders

– – – – – Borders of
former colonies

North Carolina

South
Carolina

N

Miles

0   50   100   150

0   100   200

Kilometers

Georgia

*ATLANTIC
OCEAN*

A Maryland gentleman promised female servants "have the best luck here . . . for they are no sooner on shoar, but they are courted into . . . Matrimony."

And from the southern colonies of North and South Carolina came word that single women "will think themselves in the Golden Age." As one writer promised, "If they be but civil, and under 50 years of Age, some honest Man . . . will purchase them for their Wives."

"ROOTING IN THE GROUND"

The colonies needed industrious, willing hands in a land where endless labor was a fact of life. There was simply too much land, too much work, and far too few workers.

Nowhere was this more true than in the Chesapeake colonies of Virginia and Maryland (the Chesapeake). Here, most people grew tobacco, their chief cash crop, and corn, the staple of their diets. By the 1630s, more than one million pounds of tobacco sailed for Europe each year. Forty years later, the volume had increased to twenty million pounds.

Growing tobacco was backbreaking work. In the spring, tobacco seedlings required planting by hand in rows. Through the summer, workers weeded, hoed, and battled worms that could consume the crop. In fall they harvested, cured, and packed the leaves for sale.

Few English-born women had labored daily in the fields back home. To them, "rooting in the ground about Tobacco like Swine" seemed a very uncivilized way to live. But England offered few job opportunities, and most people there would never have a chance to own land. With prospects brighter in the New World, some women and men were willing to uproot and replant across the Atlantic Ocean.

INDENTURED SERVANTS

Many young people signed over their labor in a written contract called an indenture. They agreed to toil for a master in the New World for a set number of years. In exchange, they received a ticket, paid in full, for passage on a ship to the colonies. More than 80 percent of

This illustration from a seventeenth-century cookbook shows indentured servants at work in the kitchen of their master. The women performed many duties in addition to cooking.

immigrants to the Chesapeake in the 1600s (roughly 150,000 people) came as indentured servants. Males outnumbered women at least three to one. Once arrived, indentured servants owed their master four to seven years of work. During that time they could not marry.

The master, his family, and his servants usually lived together in a few crowded rooms, "the meanest Cottages in England," wrote one man in 1622, "being every ways equall (if not superior)" with the best homes in Virginia. Not until 1655 could a visitor label Virginia's homes "delightfull," if small. With everyone needed "to make a Cropp," the master, as well as his wife and children, often labored in the fields alongside their male and female servants.

Servants formed a circle of companionship. Sunday afternoons were a time of play. Men and women engaged in drinking, pipe smoking, and gambling at cards and dice. Alehouses served up a brisk business. Black men and women made up a minority of indentured servants, and the races and the sexes mingled. "We and the Negroes both alike did fare," reported one servant, "of work and food we had an equal share."

If a male servant survived the hard work and rough conditions of his indenture, he could build a new life in the colonies. A lucky few bought land or were granted a parcel of land. Most married. Meanwhile, women servants shared in the men's luck. "Maid servants of good honest stock," reported a Virginia planter in 1649, "may choose their husbands out of the better sort of people."

"SHE DESERVES TWO OR THREE BLOWES"

Servants complained, however, of "too much worke, and too little Victuals [food]," noted master William Stephens. They bemoaned the hot sun, insect bites, loneliness, and primitive living conditions. The new climate and exhausting drudgery left many servants sick. Only half of a farm's workers might be fit for duty at any one time. After a day's toil, many still faced hours of grinding corn to make their bread, described as "beating at the mortar."

When a master or mistress spoke, a servant was supposed to act without complaint or question. Yet sometimes servants sassed back or lied. Some became, as one master claimed, "more and more troublesome," marrying secretly, stealing food or other goods, or running away. One woman ran away forty times. For "saucy," lazy, or otherwise ill-behaved servants, few punishments were off limits. Whippings, beatings, and withholding food were common.

English indentured servants did have some rights in court. In 1649 Mistress Deborah Fernehaugh beat her "mayd servant" Charity Dallen till the poor girl's head was "as soft as a sponge." In a rare decision, the court protected Charity by ordering that her indenture be sold to another master or mistress. Mistress Fernehaugh was fined.

Some masters tried to extend the time of servitude. A simple charge of "unruliness" was enough to legally tack time onto an indenture. Anne Thompson had already served six years when her master sold her indenture shortly before his death. Her new master kept Anne working for three more years, well beyond her original agreement. Anne's brother petitioned the Maryland court in 1661 for her freedom. Few servants used the courts, however, fearing worse treatment if they lost their case.

Indentured servants were not allowed to marry. Yet some female servants got pregnant. Virginia lawmakers noted in 1662 "that some dissolute [immoral] masters have gotten their maides with child." Time lost from work due to pregnancy and childbearing was added to a woman's term of indenture. A woman owed this extra time, even if she had been sexually abused by her master. In this case, the parish church (rather than the master) was awarded the extra work from the woman—two years' worth.

An indentured servant pleads her case before the court of the Massachusetts Bay Colony. Under the pressure of strict laws and social sentiment, it took great courage for women to speak in court.

Some women became desperate. Elizabeth Greene was the sole female in a household of males in the 1660s. When Greene became pregnant, she feared added years to her indenture and claimed a miscarriage. But the courts charged her with killing her baby and hanged her in 1664.

A CHANCE IN NEW ENGLAND

Compared to the Chesapeake, New England relied less on indentured servants. The area's economy didn't depend on a labor-intensive crop like tobacco, which gobbled up workers. In addition, many Puritan officials frowned on the crude behavior of servants, "both men and womenkind." Indentured servants were felt to be too "idle" for Puritan tastes, and too disrespectful, especially toward Puritans' idea of God. Besides, New Englanders preferred the labor of their own large families—sons, daughters, nieces, and nephews—to the labor of a suspicious lot of strangers. Many New England sons still worked for their fathers even after becoming adults. Daughters worked at home until they married.

Indentured servants in New England faced a better chance of charting a successful future life than their counterparts in the South. New England servants generally served less time (three to four years). More of them received training in craft skills, or perhaps even learned to read. New England's economy was strong and growing. When their indentures ended, servants could farm, fish, trade, or keep a shop.

A SHIFT IN LABOR

In the closing decades of the 1600s, the flood of indentured servants ebbed. The economic situation in England improved, and fewer young people felt pressure to leave. With fewer servants available in the colonies, those who did come could strike better terms. Newer colonies (such as Pennsylvania, founded in 1681) offered enticements such as shorter terms of work.

England gladly sent undesirable people to the colonies as indentured servants. It relocated highwaymen, pickpockets, cutthroats, prostitutes, and rebels from Scotland and Ireland. Even orphans were routinely shipped to the colonies as indentured servants. But even more workers were needed.

By the mid-1600s, white legislators passed new laws that reshaped the lives of black people in the colonies. Carolina, copying the labor system in the West Indies, already depended mostly on enslaved blacks for work. The greatest changes came in the Chesapeake colonies of Virginia and Maryland. In one example, the Maryland General Assembly passed "An Act Concerning Negroes & Other Slaves" in September 1664. This law declared that any blacks brought into the colony would now automatically serve for life. All children born to a slave also became slaves for life. Any free Englishwoman who, "to the disgrace of our Nation doe intermarry with Negro Slaves," would also become a slave and serve her husband's master.

In 1667 Virginians took up the issue of whether or not a master had to free enslaved children who had been baptized as Christians. They decided to close this path to freedom. Baptizing an enslaved child, proclaimed the new law, "doth not alter the condition of the person as to his bondage or freedome."

Ann Joice, an indentured black woman, was one victim of these changing laws. In 1668 Joice sailed from England to Maryland, where she worked as a cook. When her indenture expired, her master, Henry Darnall, simply refused to free her. He flung her indenture papers into the fire. Without her papers, and with the new laws defining slavery, Ann Joice had no legal rights to help her. As if to underscore his power, her master imprisoned her in a cellar for five or six months. Years later, her enslaved grandson recalled his grandmother's helpless rage: "If she had her just right that she ought to be free and all her children."

By 1672 free blacks in the Chesapeake had lost their right to carry a weapon. They could no longer hire white servants to work for them. And by 1705, free blacks had lost their right to testify in a court of law.

Some slaves, including mothers and their children, jumped overboard from slave ships. They chose the near certainty of drowning over enslavement.

"PERPETUAL SERVITUDE"

To fill the growing demand for slaves, slave traders sailed to communities in Africa and ripped tens of thousands of Africans from their families. They crammed the captives into ships as breathing cargo. During the filthy, suffocating voyage—called the Middle Passage—captives lay chained in rows, with as much room as a corpse in a coffin. Nearly one-fifth of them died during the trip.

Survivors arrived in the New World weak, sick, and drenched in fear. More died during their first weeks anchored in harbor, as they were waiting to be sold. To the captives, the buyers boarding the slave ships were strangers speaking foreign words and wearing unfamiliar clothes.

The strangers jabbed and inspected the Africans, then led them away into an alien, frightening world. The people who were not sold sailed to the next port. The process continued for about two months as the slavers made their profit.

In Africa, a young woman had been a daughter, a wife, a mother, a sister, and an aunt. In the colonies, she was connected to no one. Homesickness, grief over the loss of her family, terror: All these ached in her bones. Once she arrived at the farm that would be her new home, she might be the only African woman there. Creating a new family or community such as she'd known in Africa was impossible.

She was quickly sent to the tobacco or rice fields, where she learned how to work to avoid punishment. Her master controlled her life. She listened carefully, trying to grasp words in his language. She even had to learn the new name he gave her.

Enslaved African American women work a field several months after being snatched away from their lives and families in Africa.

One out of every four new slaves died during their first year in the colonies. Most lived on small plantations with few other blacks. All slaves lived and worked under the watch of their white owners. Eventually a slave woman might wed an African man on a nearby farm. Because establishing a family was so difficult.

"FORBIDDEN LIBERTY"

The demand for labor grew continually, and the slave trade expanded. Enslaved people were sold as laborers all along the Atlantic seaboard. The number of blacks in Virginia rose from about three hundred in 1650 to about three thousand in 1680. Between 1700 and 1740, fifty-four thousand black people were brought to the Chesapeake as slaves. Forty-nine thousand of them came directly from Africa.

White colonists needing workers viewed slavery as an economic bargain. Where indentured servants worked for a limited time, enslaved laborers worked for life. Where white servants could protest their treatment in court, slaves had no rights in court or anywhere.

Many white people eventually came to see blacks as inferior to themselves. They believed black people could get by with less food, clothing, and shelter. A slave might die of exhaustion. But no Englishman should have to spend his days "labouring in the Corn or rice field, Broiling in the Sun, Pale and Fainting under the Excessive heat."

Slave owners mostly wanted male workers. But a woman was valuable, too. Her children automatically belonged to her master. "It is therefore advantageous to have Negro women," a Swedish visitor explained. Sometimes the master himself made his slave women pregnant in order to increase his number of slaves.

A healthy black woman almost always worked in the fields. As more and more black women did farmwork, fewer and fewer white women were needed in the fields. "Sufficient Distinction is also made between the Female-Servants, and Slaves," wrote Robert Beverly in the early 1700s, "for a White Woman is rarely or never put to work in the Ground, if she be good for anything else."

African American slaves process tobacco, **background.** *Colonial tobacco plantations could not operate without the labor of free and enslaved women.*

Most northern slaveholders owned only one or two slaves, and fewer slaves lived in the North overall. Northern slaves worked in less brutal conditions. They did a wider range of jobs. A slave woman might cook, clean, spin thread, or watch her master's children. Slaves in cities such as Philadelphia and New York organized churches and formed communities with other blacks.

Solidarity among slaves, however, made white colonists uneasy. The slaves' "continual aspiring after their forbidden Liberty, renders them Unwilling servants," wrote Massachusetts judge Samuel Sewall in 1700. Slave uprisings were rare, but violent. Black women as well as men were arrested in an uprising in New York in 1712. The Stono Revolt in South Carolina was especially shocking. It began in September 1739 when twenty black Carolinians seized guns and gunpowder from a local store. The band grew to more than one hundred as the rebels headed south, burning houses and killing whites who tried to stop them. By the time the revolt ended, twenty whites and forty blacks lay dead.

UP TO THEIR ELBOWS IN HOUSEWIFERY

Pease porridge hot,
Pease porridge cold,
Pease porridge in the pot,
Nine days old!
  —from an old English nursery rhyme

She rose at dawn and put on layers of long, heavy petticoats over her shift. Then she tied an apron around her waist and wound her hair up inside a linen cap. Perhaps her house had two rooms below and two rooms up and sat on a dusty town street. In a shop attached to the house, her seafaring husband sold a variety of useful goods.

Or maybe she lived on a farm. She had a smaller house with a kitchen across the back, a dairy barn, and a smokehouse. Or she lived on the far reaches of the wooded frontier in a one-room cabin with a storage loft above and a lean-to shelter for her animals.

Wherever she lived, she rose at dawn and began a dizzying whirl of daily chores. Her family's survival often depended upon her skills and efforts.

KEEPING THE KETTLE FILLED

The house and yard—including the dairy barn, kitchen garden, pig-sty, and hen house—served as the workplace for most colonial women. Preparing food consumed much of a woman's day. In the gray morning chill, she reached beneath her hens and gathered fresh-laid eggs. She crouched on a milking stool next to her cow, listening to the rhythmic hiss of warm milk ricocheting off the inside of her pail. She picked an apron full of vegetables and herbs from her kitchen garden, then hurried inside to begin breakfast. She might fry some cornmeal, or slice bread served with butter and cold, leftover meat.

Dinner, served at midday, was the largest meal. Many women cooked a "pottage"—a simple one-pot meal of meat or fish boiled with cabbage, beans, and other vegetables. Families rounded out the meal with cheese and bread, washed down with hearty mugfuls of home-brewed beer. For most people, supper was a frugal meal—a slice of bread, a cup of milk. The poorer families lived mostly on baked and boiled cornmeal flavored with a bit of bacon or salted beef. The poorest families might skip supper altogether.

In contrast, a wealthy woman could provide a sumptuous spread. Her servants did the work. A visitor in one Virginia home described "tables fournished with porke, kidd [young goat], chickens, turkeys, young geese . . . besides plentie of milk, cheese, butter, and corn."

Cooking required muscle. Women churned cream into butter. They squeezed whey from cheese. They lifted heavy iron pots. They hauled buckets of water from wells or springs.

To cook, a woman stood in a large fireplace—even in summer's heat—with her skirts tucked up for safety. She cooked over several fires, coaxing banked embers or piles of red hot coals into low flames. She determined just when the brick oven was hot enough to bake bread by thrusting her arm inside it, then counting how long she could stand the heat.

A woman's labor transformed milk and rennet (the lining from a calf's stomach) into cheese. She brewed a watered-down "small beer" several times a month. "Strong beer" was brewed in October.

The "singing of the cider" as mashed apples fermented and hissed was another song for autumn. From her slaughtered pigs, she stuffed sausages and pickled and smoked cuts of meat.

Always, she kept an eye on stocking her shelves with supplies for winter, when fresh food grew scarce. When Beatrice Plummer's husband died in 1672, the Newbury, Massachusetts, court made an inventory of his farm. The list included provisions Beatrice had stored away for winter. She'd salted and smoked four and a half sides of bacon. She'd turned pails of milk into twenty-eight pounds of cheese and four pounds of butter. She'd gathered twenty-five bushels of grain (barley, oats, wheat, and rye) for future baking and brewing. She'd harvested and dried bushels of peas and beans. She'd brewed a barrel of cider. She'd grown and harvested sacks of cabbages and turnips. She had also purchased, or traded for, quantities of sugar, spices, and molasses.

One seventeenth-century New England woman claimed that a wife "utterly ignorant" in food skills could only perform half her marriage vow. "She may love and obey," wrote the woman, "but she cannot cherish, serve, and keep him with that true duty which is ever expected."

"NO SOONER COME, BUT GONE"

A woman battled her family's sickness and injuries armed with minerals (such as iron), herbs, tree bark, and even sheep's dung. She worked her cures through homemade potions, brewed teas, and rubbed-on salves.

Without refrigeration, food spoiled, and many people suffered from stomach ailments. They also fell ill with contagious smallpox, measles, diphtheria, influenza, malaria, and pneumonia. There was little anyone could do to treat these deadly diseases. Smallpox was the colonies' greatest killer. In the 1720s, an inoculation to prevent smallpox was introduced with some success. Many colonists remained suspicious of the procedure, however, since it involved scooping pus from an infected person and scratching it into the skin of a healthy person.

A mother mourns the death of her child. Colonial women were frequently faced with death and loss.

Death plagued colonial households. Many mothers buried children younger than five. Many buried still more children before their youngsters reached adulthood. Anne Bradstreet wrote a poem when her infant grandson, Simon, died. It began with words so many parents echoed: "No sooner come, but gone."

SHIRTS AND SHIFTS

Making clothes was another time-consuming chore for colonial women. Sometimes the process started from scratch, with shearing sheep's wool. Following the shearing, a woman washed, carded, and combed the wool. Then she spun it into skeins of thread, dipped the skeins into home-made dyes, and wove the threads into fabric on her loom. From sheepshearing to sewn shirt required nearly a year of work. Many women could not afford their own spinning wheel or loom. They traded goods or labor for the fabric needed to sew clothes—or paid scarce cash.

To make linen, a colonial woman planted and raised flax. She cut the grown plants, soaked and dried them, then pounded the stalks to break down the tough plant fibers. Next the fibers were spun, dyed, and woven into linen. Women used linen to sew shirts and shifts

A colonial woman stands at her hearth boiling clothes to wash them while tending to her baby.

(underclothes) as well as aprons, caps, and baby dresses. Luxuries such as tablecloths, napkins, and sheets were also sewn from linen.

A woman hired a tailor or dressmaker to sew fitted dress tops, jackets, and men's breeches. Wealthier women bought material from England. Many southern women ordered fabric from English stores when the tobacco crop shipped for sale. Nearly all women handled a needle, thread, and thimble with skill. Each tiny stitch on every garment, yards and yards of fabric, was sewn by hand. Sewing, mending, or altering their family's clothes was a constant chore. Women also knitted stockings and caps.

Since clothes were expensive and time consuming to make, most colonists owned a very limited wardrobe. Only the wealthy could afford yards of lace, fancy buttons, or embroidery silks that set their clothes above the common folk.

A woman also counted laundry among her chores, washing the family's linens (about once a month) and infant's diapers. She scrubbed clothes stooped over a washtub, filled with water she had lugged from a well or stream and heated over a fire. After wringing each piece by hand, she hung the clothes to dry in the hot summer breeze or to freeze-dry in the winter cold. Laundry chores didn't end until she pressed her clothes with a heavy wedge of iron heated in her fireplace. Clothes made from wool or expensive fabrics like silks were not washed, for fear they'd be ruined. Dirty garments and seldom-washed bodies did not make for sweet-smelling colonists.

HELPING HANDS

Whenever possible, women enlivened their drudgery by sharing. They organized corn-husking and quilting parties. They competed to see who could pick the most berries or spin the most thread. Swapping news and refreshments added fun.

Many women saved work by bartering goods and services. Goodwife Smith might swap a crock of churned butter for some soap

Colonial women often worked together to ease the burden of their chores. The women shown above are making soap.

boiled up by Goodwife Jones. Women also turned to their daughters for help. As a girl helped, she learned skills she would need as an adult. Colonel William Byrd, a wealthy Virginian, wrote about his daughters in 1727, "They are every day up to their Elbows in House-wifery," he said, "which will qualify them . . . for useful Wives and if they live long enough, for Notable Women."

Women living on small farms or on the frontier continued working in the field, as well as tending to household jobs. All women juggled their chores with the needs of infants, toddlers, and children. Many complained that their lives possessed a weary sameness throughout the year.

An idle housewife was a disgrace. Readers might have wondered when Anne Bradstreet had found time to write her book of poetry *The Tenth Muse.* In the preface, her brother-in-law assured them that Anne hadn't neglected her duties to loll about writing poems. "These poems are the fruit but of some few houres," he claimed, "curtailed [stolen] from her sleep and other refreshments."

In addition to her duties as a housewife, Anne Bradstreet, left, made time to write. Her writings, published during a time when female writers were rare, help people understand colonial America.

EARNING HER KEEP

Colonial women earned income or goods in a variety of ways. Women—especially widows—often took in boarders, for example. A town woman might help run the family shop. She could cut back on gardening by buying produce from farm women who brought their surpluses to town. When possible, she hired other women to cook and wash clothes.

Many young women lived as servants in the homes of wealthy families. Colonial families were often large, and sometimes food was scarce. Poor parents saved money by sending a daughter to live and work in someone else's home.

Women transformed other housewifery skills into income. Lydia Dyar advertised flower and vegetable seeds for sale in the *Boston Evening Post.* Mary Crathorne ran advertisements in the *Pennsylvania Gazette* announcing that she sold bottled mustards, raisins, and pickles. Women earned money as dressmakers and hatmakers. They washed clothes and starched laces. They sold fine needlework as bed hangings and cushions. "Sister Bradish" was a baker, brewer, and comforter to homesick Harvard students in the 1650s. A woman known only as Mistress Hewlett of Ipswich ran a poultry business and loaned her husband money. Legally, all her earnings belonged to him, but Mr. Hewlett commented, "I meddle not with the geese nor the turkeys For they are hers for she has been and is a good wife to me."

Female tavern-keepers were common. Taverns hummed as noisy gathering spots, a source of news and gossip. Jane Vobe owned the King's Arms Tavern in Virginia's capital city, Williamsburg. Vobe and her staff served food and drink, provided lodging, managed a lost-and-found, and sold theater tickets. Another enterprising innkeeper capitalized on her strategic location at a river crossing in Maryland. Remembered simply as Mrs. Fenwick, she was paid five hundred pounds of tobacco for "her trouble and charge in entertaining and setting people over the river." In the 1730s, another female innkeeper enticed customers to a dance at her inn by offering a raffle. The prize was "a Virginia Negro woman fit for house business and her child."

Some women earned cash or goods as midwives and nurses. Elizabeth Girandeau of South Carolina advertised she would take in persons recovering from smallpox inoculations. "The best attendance will be given," she promised. Women also sold homemade remedies, claiming their concoctions cured everything from eye ailments to infestations of worms.

And women continued to be a steadying influence on men. When James Oglethorpe founded Georgia, the last of the thirteen colonies, in 1733, he advertised for wives for his soldiers. Married men, he noted, proved "the most industrious, and willing to plant" roots in American soil.

LEADING ROLES

In Maryland, Margaret Brent remained unmarried, a so-called "spinster," so she could control her own business and land. Mistress Brent also wanted her share of control in government matters. When she boldly asked the legislature to grant her a vote, her request was quickly squashed. According to the Maryland Assembly record, "The said Mistress Brent [then] protested against all proceedings in this present Assembly, unless she may be present and vote." In 1647 Maryland's governor named the feisty Brent an executor of his will.

Margaret Hardenbroeck settled in New Amsterdam in 1659 and ran a successful shipping and trade business. She was one of about 134 women involved in business in the Dutch colony. After the English took over the colony in 1664, their laws forbade Margaret from owning property or purchasing goods in her own name. Only her husband had that power. By Margaret's death in 1691, the number of women business owners in New York had shrunk dramatically—down to 43.

Forty years later, in January 1733, a revolutionary spirit stirred the widowed businesswomen of New York. "We are House Keepers, Pay our Taxes, carry on Trade, and most of us are She Merchants," they explained in the *New York Journal,* "and as we in some measure contribute to the Support of Government, we ought to be Intitled to some of the Sweets of it; but we find ourselves entirely neglected."

Outspoken and self-assured, Margaret Brent speaks before the Maryland Assembly.

Some women carried on family businesses after a husband's death. In 1738 Elizabeth Timothy announced she would take over publication of the *South Carolina Gazette.* She hoped her husband's subscribers would "be kindly pleased to continue their Favours...to his poor afflicted Widow with six small Children and another hourly expected."

Like men in business, women often petitioned the courts to help collect what customers owed. In 1765 shop owner Agnes Lind advertised that "all persons indebted to her are desired to pay off their accounts, especially those of two or three years standing, otherwise they may expect to find them in the hands of an attorney at law."

Yet women like Agnes Lind were relatively rare. Most colonial women knew little about business and had merely a smidgen of education. Only a few—maybe 30 percent—could read or write (about half the percentage of literate males). In general, people viewed education for females as dangerous. Schooling was better left to men, "whose minds are stronger."

DAUGHTERS OF EVE

Read often the Matrimonial Service, and overlook not the important word OBEY.
—advice to wives from the *Virginia Gazette*, 1737

In 1687 Sarah Harrison and Doctor James Blair stood in front of a minister reciting their marriage vows. The minister came to the place in the vows where wives promised to obey their husbands. But when he asked Sarah if she promised to obey her husband, she quietly answered, "No *obey*." In disbelief, the minister repeated the vow. Three times Sarah refused to say the word *obey*. Finally the exasperated clergyman turned to Sarah's groom. Doctor Blair nodded his permission. The wedding continued while the bride's glaring omission filled the air.

Sarah Harrison's response was shocking. From childhood on, a girl learned she must one day meekly obey her husband. In the 1600s and 1700s, marriage and childbirth were viewed as a woman's very purpose on earth.

"ONE PERSON IN THE LAW"

A single woman could sue and be sued in court. She could make contracts, earn wages, and run a business. A single woman could own and sell property. She could leave her property to her heirs.

A married woman, however, was swallowed whole into her husband's identity. The colonies were governed by English law. And English law declared that "the very being or legal existence of the woman is suspended during the marriage." Her life was "consolidated into that of the husband; under whose wing, protection, and cover, she performs everything." All that a wife possessed, right down to her shift and corset, belonged to her husband.

No law made husbands and wives share. But most people believed that marriage involved a sharing of duties. The husband provided a home, financial support, and protection. A wife ran her husband's home efficiently, raised his children, comforted him, and assisted him in all things.

Although a wife could give advice, her husband made all decisions. She had to submit to his choices. That's what the Bible taught, and most colonists were devout Christians. According to the Bible, the first man, Adam, "ruled over" his wife, Eve. Thomas Dudley reminded his daughter Mercy of this. God "gracyously placed thy good husband here," he told her, for her to "submytt and trust." John Winthrop wrote:

> The woman's own choice makes such a man her husband,
> yet being so chosen, he is her lord and She is to be subject
> to him, yet in a way of liberty, not of bondage, and a true
> wife accounts her subjection her honor and freedom.

A husband was expected to treat his wife with respect and not rule as a tyrant, even if the law said he could. She was expected to submit to him, not because he forced her, but because she chose to follow God's path.

Many couples, such as John and Margaret Winthrop, believed that spiritual and physical oneness created an ideal marriage. Husbands and wives should have "a special Care and Tenderness one of another," explained author Samuel Willard. Anne Bradstreet celebrated the love in her marriage through poetry. "If ever two were one, then surely we," she wrote. "If ever man were lov'd by wife, then thee."

Too much passion might not be a good thing, however. Mehitable Parkman wrote her husband in the late 1600s, "Mrs. Mechison tells me often she fears that I love you more than god."

FEMALES AND SIN

Marriage was the rock of a stable society. It created order and provided restraints. For that reason, everyone had a duty to marry. Maryland even taxed bachelors. An unmarried woman not only failed in her duties but also added to her parents' burdens as they continued to feed and clothe her.

The Bible taught that Eve had seduced Adam into sin by offering him a forbidden apple in the Garden of Eden. To colonists, it seemed Eve's action had branded women as troublemakers and temptresses. The "Daughters of Eve" in colonial America were depicted in books and sermons as "the weaker vessel." Women were supposed to be easily misled, tempted by flattery, and given to extravagance. People acknowledged that men contributed to sin, too. But men's sins often happened when they were enticed by females—or under the influence of alcohol.

One popular book of the early 1700s was written by a father for his daughter. According to his fatherly wisdom, men had "the larger share of Reason bestow'd upon them." A man's reason (his intellect) was necessary to guide a woman's actions. "Your *Sex* wanteth our *Reason* for your *Conduct*," this father explained. A woman also required a male's "*Strength* for your *Protection*." In return, a man needed a woman's "*Gentleness* to soften, and to entertain us."

Colonial citizens believed men could misbehave "with out contaminating the mind." But a woman had to be "virtuous" or else become "utterly undone." A double standard existed even for unfaithful spouses. "A woman who breaks her marriage vows," claimed one male writer, "is much more criminal than a man who does it."

COURTSHIP AND WEDDINGS

Young people courted at dances, barbecues, and get-togethers such as corn huskings and barn raisings. They met at church and at parties hosted by relatives.

Daughters from poor families, without money or land at stake, had the freedom to follow their hearts when choosing a husband. In wealthy families, however, parents took an active role in screening their daughter's suitors. A young woman, easily swayed by roguish flattery, could never judge a man's true character, parents believed. They wanted to ensure she would gain—and certainly not lose—by her marriage.

Often a courtship did not begin until the two fathers exchanged letters detailing financial information. Wealthy parents scrutinized the bank accounts, property, and family connections of their daughter's suitor. They told the other family up front what their daughter would receive as a marriage portion (the money or property her father would give when she married). Colonial newspapers broadcast the juicy details. In 1749 the *South Carolina Gazette* reported that Susannah Seabrook was "endowed with all agreeable Accomplishments and a Fortune of £15,000 [British pounds sterling]."

When selecting a husband, a daughter usually obeyed her parents' wishes. She greeted a marriage proposal with dignity, words of gratitude, and a firm reminder that she must consult her parents. Some colonial fathers disinherited children who married against their wishes.

If a girl didn't like her parents' choice, she had a duty to speak up. Otherwise she risked being a disloyal wife in the future. "They that marry where they affect [love] not," went a Puritan saying, "will affect [love] where they marry not."

A young woman was allowed to flirt, but she had better also wear an air of modesty sweet as any perfume. One magazine writer offered

A young couple celebrates their marriage with a traditional dance in the 1700s. Marriage was an occasion for festivity in some of the colonies.

advice about how a girl could keep from appearing unladylike—even if her heart was crying "yes!" "A virtuous woman should reject the first offer of marriage," observed the author. But the young lady shouldn't say "no" to the same man too often. As the author put it, "I would advise [not] to persist in refusing what they secretly approve."

Most weddings were simple affairs. They took place in the bride's home or maybe at her church. A frolic of food, drink, and dancing followed the ceremony. Weddings were even simpler in Puritan New England. There, marriage was merely a civil contract, not a religious rite. So Puritan weddings were officiated by a judge or a magistrate instead of a clergyman.

YOUNGER BRIDES, LARGER FAMILIES

In the early days of the colonies, many women had to serve an indenture before they could wed. By the time their indenture ended, some were already twenty-five, or even older. This was an old age for a first marriage, especially with odds high that a woman of this era would die by the age of thirty-five. Especially in the disease-infested Chesapeake colonies, many New World women bore fewer than four children before they died—a small number in this era.

In the early years of the colonial era, enslaved African women also bore few children. Some refused to bear children in an alien, harsh world. Many of them suffered from exhaustion and malnutrition, which affected their ability to bear children. Many women lived on farms with few other African Americans, limiting their choice of partners.

By the 1700s, however, times were changing for black and white women. Life expectancy for women stretched. Fewer females had indentures to serve. Many black women had not been taken from Africa, but instead, had been born in America. Young women of both races began to marry at a younger age. In fact, many eighteenth-century women wed by their sixteenth birthday.

Early marriages became so common that a female was "reckoned a stale maid" by age twenty-five. Wealthy planter William Byrd labeled his twenty-year-old daughter Evelyn an "antique virgin."

Colonial families feared that their daughters would die "old maids," alone and without children. Stereotypical images of "stale maids" and "old maids," such as the one at right, circulated throughout the colonies.

The jabs at unmarried women continued throughout the eighteenth century. Newspapers depicted "old Maids" as being jealous of every married woman. One newspaper stingingly summed up the situation. "An old maid is one of the most cranky, ill-natured, maggotty, peevish . . . good for nothing creatures . . . ," it declared. "[She] enters the world to take up room, not to make room for others."

On the other hand, women who married in the 1700s—and married early—could expect to bear many children. With no birth control available, they had to "make room" for more.

THE MOMENT OF TRAVAIL

Most eighteenth-century women spent their adult lives in a cycle of pregnancy, childbirth, and nursing. It was not uncommon for a woman to have ten to twenty pregnancies. Many women were still having babies even after their grown daughters had begun bearing children.

People explained women's labor pains as God's punishment of Eve. They quoted from the book of Genesis in the Bible: "In sorrow thou shalt bring forth children." A woman shouldn't complain of her suffering, wrote one minister. Instead, she should accept that "the Sin of my Mother [Eve], which is also my Sin, has brought all this upon me."

During and after delivery, some women died from complications such as bleeding and infection. Some were just worn out, weakened from their numerous pregnancies. When Anne Bradstreet thought about the approaching birth of one of her children, she wondered whether she would live through the delivery. "How soon, my Dear, death may my steps attend," she wrote to her husband.

Tombstone inscriptions and newspaper notices recounted many sad tales. "Died in Child Birth in the 33d Year of her age, Mrs. Sarah Carlyle." "Of a Miscarriage of Twins, died here in the 24th Year of her age . . . Mrs. Calhoun." "Underneath lies what was mortal of Mrs. Margaret Edwards. . . . She Died in Travail [labor] with her tenth Child Aged 34 years."

Mrs. Freake holds her daughter, Baby Mary. With limited medical knowledge, childbirth and child rearing could be treacherous times for mothers and their children.

Going into labor was "being brought to bed," "lying in," or arriving at "the moment of travail." Women in labor relied on other women for comfort and help. A midwife, experienced in matters of birth, attended the mother. Some midwives delivered hundreds of babies during their careers. Female relatives and friends also helped, passing the time by munching "groaning cakes" and sipping "groaning beer." Husbands played no part other than running errands and waiting.

Since a woman's main duty was to bear children, the best mothers were those with the most offspring. Anne Bradstreet was childless during the first eight years of her marriage. Many years later, after raising eight healthy children, she recalled those earlier dark days. "It pleased God to keep me a long time without a child," she wrote, "which was a great grief to me and cost me many prayers and tears."

Wealthy women had servants to help with childcare and housework. But most women returned to household duties shortly after delivery.

Eventually, as new members were added to a growing family, older children helped their mothers with young ones.

Society viewed mothers as the indulgent parent—which was not recognized as a good thing. For balance, children required a father's guidance and discipline. In reality, however, many mothers were so busy with constant chores that they had little time either to spoil or discipline individual children. Only the wealthiest women, like Eliza Lucas of South Carolina, could study books on child rearing and create plans for the education of their children.

"NOW WIVES"

Dangers in childbirth, rampant disease, deadly accidents, and exhausting work meant death was part of everyday life in the colonies. A wife or husband might die at any time. But society was built on marriage and the sharing of duties. Not surprisingly, most people remarried after the loss of a spouse. Marrying five or six times was not uncommon. And remarriages often occurred quite quickly. In one breath, people offered sympathy for the loss of a spouse. In the next, they gave congratulations on a new marriage.

A woman known only as Thomasine, a widow with three children, married Virginian John Thruston. Over the next sixteen years, she bore sixteen more children. Nine of her children died before their fifteenth birthday. Thomasine herself died two weeks after delivering her nineteenth baby. Six weeks later, John remarried. He fathered eight more children with his second wife.

A father might remarry so often that his children referred to his "now wife." Mothers facing deadly illness or childbirth worried that a stepmother might neglect the children left behind. Writing of her own possible death, Anne Bradstreet begged her husband to protect their children from "step Dame's injury."

With resources often scarce, some stepmothers treated stepchildren as mere servants or banished them elsewhere to work. The rightful heir to the father's land, money, and goods was often disputed by the children of his several wives.

"NAUGHTY FURIOUS HOUSEWIVES"

Although wives were taught to obey their husbands, they didn't always do so. Husbands did not always treat their spouses with respect. Colonial mates sometimes argued, criticized, and ignored each other.

In 1744 Susannah Cooper petitioned the Virginia government for help. She had not heard from her runaway husband in twenty years. She claimed the fellow had spent all the money she'd brought to their marriage. Even though legally she remained a married woman, she asked the assembly members to grant her the right to sell property, make contracts, and provide for herself. In this case, the members agreed to her petition.

Susannah Cooper had not sought a divorce. Divorce was rarely an option. Between 1664 and 1775, no divorce was granted in New York. In South Carolina, only the governor and his council could dissolve a marriage. In New England, divorce was slightly easier since marriage was viewed as a civil contract. Most often courts ordered battling couples to reform and behave, even in cases where husbands physically abused their wives.

No one questioned that children belonged to the father. Elizabeth Byrd was heartsick when her husband sent their baby to live with his meddling mother. "Poor dear babe. . . ," wrote Elizabeth. "But Sir, your Orders must be obeyed whatever reluctance I find thereby."

With so few options, some women "eloped" (fled) from their husbands. Newspapers frequently carried notices from husbands who rushed to announce they would no longer pay an eloped wife's debts. One declared his wife was "highly undutiful and disaffectionate." Worse was the woman who had become a "naughty furious Housewife." Some abandoned husbands accused their wives of stealing their own dresses and petticoats when they left. Most insisted they had no idea why a wife had fled.

Some wives returned the favor. "John Cantwell has the impudence to advertise me in the Papers," wrote wife Sarah of South Carolina, "cautioning all Persons against crediting me; he never had any Credit till he married me...: I never eloped, I went away before his Face when he beat me."

PROVIDING FOR A WIFE

When their husband died, many women temporarily gained control of the family finances. A wife was legally entitled to one-third of her husband's estate. In addition, a husband usually left his wife her jewelry in his will. Typically he gave her the use of their home until her own death. Sometimes she ruled as homeowner only until her oldest son turned twenty-one and took over.

If the couple had young children when the father died, guardianship might be granted to the mother. But it might be given instead to a male relative or a friend of the father.

If a widow remarried, her new husband not only took over the former husband's estate but also controlled her "thirds." George Washington became a wealthy man when he married the recently widowed Martha Custis. Many husbands made provisions for a wife's remarriage. "My wife Alice to Have and enjoy the Land I live on for her widowhood," wrote Mathias Marriott of Virginia in his will. "After her death or remarriage the Land is to return to my son."

Some husbands rewarded their wives for a lifetime of loyalty. Benjamin Harrison, a signer of the Declaration of Independence, left his wife more than her thirds. "She hath at all times behaved in a most dutiful...manner to me and all ways been assisting through my whole affairs," Harrison explained. Samuel Cobb, a poor Virginia farmer, could not provide for both his wife and his grown children. As many husbands did, he chose his wife. "I do think it my Duty to provide for a Wife now in Decline of life who so well Deserved it from me," he said.

Colonial Americans used public humiliation, such as the stocks, **above right,** *as punishment for offenses as common as gossiping.*

GOSSIPS, WITCHES, AND PUNISHMENTS

Colonial people believed in physical "correction" for wrongdoers. Depending upon a woman's crime, she faced an assortment of punishments: fines, branding, whipping, burning, and hanging.

One common crime was gossiping, which was considered a female sin. "Brabling women," read an early Virginia law, "often...scandalize their neighbors for which their poore husbands are often brought into chargeable and vexatious suites." Officials marched a gossip to the nearest pond, tied her to a stool on the end of a long wooden arm, and ducked her underwater five or six times.

Other common charges against women included bearing a child outside of marriage and having an affair. If she couldn't pay the penalty, which was typically a fine, she suffered a public whipping.

Some women were sentenced to death. Sometimes the condemned, like pirate Anne Bonney, "pleaded their bellies." By claiming to be pregnant, a woman could stall her execution. In these cases, a group of matrons examined the woman to see if she really was pregnant. If so, the execution was postponed until after the birth.

Witchcraft was a crime charged almost exclusively against women. For most of the seventeenth century, authorities only occasionally prosecuted women thought to be witches.

Witch hunts began in earnest in Salem Village, Massachusetts, in 1692. That year, the English king revoked Massachusetts Bay's charter, appointing a royal governor to rule instead. New England's population had boomed, and many of the new immigrants did not hold Puritan beliefs. Decades of frontier wars with Native Americans had also shaken

A fainting woman, **bottom center,** *points an accusing finger at an older woman,* **standing center,** *charged with practicing witchcraft.*

people's faith. Resentments festered between rural people and the merchant class, poor and rich. In Salem, tensions divided the town east and west. Society appeared in upheaval, maybe even gripped by the devil.

The accusations of witchcraft began after some girls saw the "witch's spirit" in nightmares. Seemingly under an evil spell, the girls twitched and shrieked with pain. People believed that their bewitchments were incurable until the witch was found and punished.

A witch hysteria followed, led by Puritan magistrates and clergy. Older women, many widowed and without protection, were easy marks for finger pointing. By the summer of 1692, nineteen people—fourteen of them women—had been executed as witches. The jails were filled with more than one hundred others awaiting trial.

Once in court, the judges fired questions at the accused, such as "Have you made no contact with the Devil?" Sarah Good, a homeless beggar, was asked, "Why do you hurt these children?" Sarah denied she was a witch. She claimed she had been falsely accused, but it did her little good.

As Martha Corey stood in court, the "bewitched" girls told the judges they saw the Devil whispering in Martha's ear. Then they screamed in agony as if someone tortured them. Martha Corey could only repeat, "I am an innocent person! I never had to do with witchcraft!"

Both women hanged.

As the frightening number of arrests soared, more tolerant voices raised. A few had the governor's ear. Some women newly accused of witchcraft belonged to families with enough money and influence to protect their wives and daughters. In October Governor William Phips halted further arrests. In January 1693, the remaining accused were released.

A CHANGING WORLD

I wrote my father a very long letter on his plantation affairs.
—Eliza Lucas, manager of her family's plantations in South Carolina, July 1739

In the earliest days of Jamestown and Plymouth, a few hundred people had struggled to survive in a wilderness. By the early 1700s, colonial citizens filled scores of villages and towns, and even a few thriving cities. An ever-growing network of new dirt roads linked people. Women as well as men steered rowboats along waterways, the chief highways in the colonies. As Eliza Lucas noted, "We are seventeen miles by land, and six by water from Charles Town [Charleston, South Carolina]."

"AS WELL AS MOST MEN"

As the Atlantic coast became more settled, the rough frontier crept steadily westward. Frontier life remained harsh and often lonely. A woman relied on herself to meet her family's needs. She hoed and harvested and hoisted a gun when necessary. William Byrd described one frontier woman as "a very civil woman and shews nothing of ruggedness . . . yett she will . . . perform the most manfull Exercises as well as most men."

A frontier wife owned little. Her clothes were simple and few. Her family ate their meager meals off a few wooden dishes they shared. Her home was typically one room and offered little privacy. Young George Washington described turning in for the night at a frontier home he visited in 1748. "I lay down before the fire upon a little hay . . . with man, wife, and children, like a parcel of dogs and cats," he wrote. "Happy is he, who gets the berth nearest the fire."

Frontier women also faced the brunt of warfare between colonists and Native Americans. In New England, many women were taken captive. Native Americans sometimes traded their captives for ransom money.

At other times, Native Americans adopted their captives as new members of the tribe. The women who accepted this situation and adapted to Native American life were usually young. Mary Jemison embraced her new life with the Seneca. "With them was my home," she later explained.

A colonial woman delivers gunpowder to Virginia settlers during a battle with Native Americans. Conflict increased between colonists and American Indians as the settlers pushed farther westward.

Some women struggled fiercely against their captors. The horrific story of Hannah Duston began in Haverhill, Massachusetts. As one minister recorded, Native Americans "fell upon some part of Haverhill about seven in the morning." The Native Americans "killed or carried away thirty-nine or forty persons." Hannah Duston had given birth to a baby girl only days before the attack. Duston watched as a Native American warrior swung her newborn's head into a tree, killing the child.

Along with her neighbor Mary Neff, Duston was then marched into the wilderness. One hundred miles and several weeks later, she determined she would go no farther. She grabbed a hatchet and—with help from Neff and an English boy captured earlier—Duston killed her captors as they slept.

Duston made her way back to Haverhill with ten Native American scalps. For each, she was paid twenty-five pounds sterling (English currency) by the Massachusetts legislature. Ministers in Boston compared her to Biblical heroines.

"THE ENGLISH HAVE TAKEN"

Disease. Warfare. Loss of tribal lands. The invasion of several million Europeans into the New World brought devastating consequences for Native American people. "The English have taken away great parts of their Country," wrote Robert Beverly in the early 1700s. Colonists had "introduc'd drunkeness and Luxury amongst them." Native Americans yearned for European goods and weapons, "disiring a thousand things they never dreamt of before."

At first Native Americans couldn't believe that a European would trade twenty gleaming butcher knives for one beaver skin. "The English have no sense," said one man. Native Americans played the European powers against one another, trading with the French, Dutch, Spanish, or British, depending on who offered most. When Britain drove the Dutch out of the middle colonies in the late 1600s and France out of Canada in 1763, Native Americans lost this leverage.

Native American and French forces defeat General Braddock in 1755. Native Americans allied with colonial French during the French and Indian Wars (1754–1763), hoping to oust the British from their lands.

Many fur traders improved business by marrying Native American women. A wife maintained friendly relations between her husband and her people. She also served as an interpreter. And, very importantly, she knew how to dress a skin. "Moreover," remarked Carolina trader John Lawson, "such a Man gets a great Trade with the savages."

With millions and millions of beaver, deer, fox, and otter skins traded, tribes eventually fought for control of the best fur trapping lands. The powerful Iroquois nearly destroyed tribes such as the Huron and Erie. Some tribes spent more time hunting for furs than hunting for food. Women devoted more and more days to dressing skins.

In early fall, traders advanced the hunters guns, ammunition, and food for the winter hunt. In summer, when the pelts were delivered, the hunter's debt was marked paid. Any extra income purchased more English goods: knives and hatchets, brightly colored wool, copper kettles, and jewelry.

As animals were slaughtered or migrated west, the supply of furs dwindled. Eventually Native Americans couldn't supply enough furs to cancel their debts. Some tribes, in debt to the European traders and still wanting goods, handed over precious acres of land.

The governor of South Carolina noted that his colony had once "swarmed with tribes of Indians." By 1770, "there now remain... nothing of them but their names." By the time of the American Revolution, few Native Americans lived where their ancestors had farmed and hunted for centuries. Most tribes drifted west, away from the Europeans, and kept their culture alive in new homes.

BUY, BUY, BUY

Immigrants arrived regularly from England, Ireland, Germany, Holland, Sweden, Scotland, and France. From 1720 to 1770, New England's population boomed, growing from 170,000 to 570,000. Meanwhile the southern colonies added 580,000 new people. People in the middle colonies were joined by 460,000 newcomers.

Spending cash and begging credit, this growing population improved their standard of living. Wealthy colonists ordered goods directly from England. American shops burst with English goods:

The cupboard at left contains a selection of the fine English pottery wealthy colonial women bought for their households.

china teapots, fancy fabrics, and ready-made candles and soap. Furniture makers and seamstresses copied English—and French—tastes in furniture and clothing fashions.

An average family in this era possessed luxuries only the wealthiest would have enjoyed in earlier times. Middle-class colonists dined regularly with forks, which had been rare even in well-to-do seventeenth-century homes. They ate and drank from individual plates and cups instead of sharing wooden bowls. They replaced their benches with wooden chairs. They sipped tea. And nearly everyone could buy spices or trade for them.

All this buying, however, widened the gap between rich, middle class, and poor. Americans rich from trading and planting built many-roomed mansions stuffed with costly goods. They dined at tables gleaming with china and silver. They eased into plump upholstered furniture instead of perching on hard wooden chairs. Clocks chimed the hour. Rich curtains decorated windows that gleamed with glass instead of oiled cloth. Gilt-edged books lined shelves.

Rich Americans enjoyed luxurious pastimes, too. The Reverend Johnathan Boucher looked forward to these when he visited from England. As he wrote to a friend, in Virginia "they tell me I may see . . . more brilliant assemblies [dances] than I ever c'd [could] in the North of Engl'd [England]."

"PRETTY GENTLEWOMAN"

Society expected the wife of a prosperous man to demonstrate polished grace and manners in all she did. She had to set a perfect table laden with beautifully presented dishes. The old one-dish pottage—or even one course—was no longer grand enough. Cookbooks showed her how to create complicated dishes. Even carving the main course took on added importance as a wife learned to "Thigh that Woodcock" and "Wing that Quail," "Barb that Lobster," and "Splat that Pike."

This eighteenth-century "gentlewoman" was far removed from the seventeenth-century wife. And she had little in common with women on the frontier to the west of her. A nursery rhyme defined the new ideal: "Curly locks, Curly Locks / Wilt thou be mine? / Thou shalt not wash dishes / Nor yet feed the swine / But sit on a cushion / And sew a fine seam / And feed upon strawberries / Sugar, and cream."

Benjamin Franklin wrote his sister Jane, a new bride, in 1727:

> I have been thinking what would be a suitable present for me to make. . . . I had almost determined on a tea table, but when I consider that the character of a good housewife was far preferable to that of being only a pretty gentle-woman, I concluded to send you a spinning wheel.

Even a gentlewoman was expected to work while running a thrifty household. Mary Holyoke's diary from the 1760s listed numerous house-hold chores alongside tea parties and receptions. She washed and ironed, sewed petticoats and shirts. She planted herbs and vegetables, raised poultry, salted pork, and bottled her own wine. She also shopped, laying in supplies of candles, salmon, and "77 Pounds of butter for winter."

Hosting tea parties, **right,** *was one of the duties of the colonial gentlewoman.*

This needlepoint piece depicts an enslaved African American house servant and her mistress.

Only the most financially privileged women, such as Eliza Lucas or Mrs. Robert Carter, had an army of enslaved labor to follow their orders. These women filled their days with managing their children's education and supervising workers in their gardens and homes. They also lavished money and attention on social obligations. In one year, Mrs. Carter of Nomini Hall in Virginia served her guests more than 27,000 pounds of pork, 20 head of cattle, and 150 gallons of brandy. Her household used 550 bushels of wheat and 100 pounds of flour.

ENSLAVED AMERICANS

Much of the colonies' expanding wealth, especially in the South, rested on the backs of slaves. Their numbers rose dramatically with each decade. By the 1770s, nearly 500,000 persons of African descent (some free, but most enslaved) lived in the colonies.

Enslaved black women continued working in the fields. In addition, more and more worked as house servants. Female slaves made soap, dipped candles, and wove cloth, all "under the Eye of the Mistress," as one observer put it.

In the 1700s, black women living on large plantations could create a real sense of family for themselves. Instead of being isolated like slave women of earlier times, they connected to a web of relationships. A black woman could be wife, mother, daughter, sister, niece, and aunt.

Slaves could not *legally* marry. But many pledged their love to one another. Husbands and wives who lived on different farms kept their bond alive through visits. Many stole moments for secret meetings.

In addition, a slave mother was usually allowed to keep her youngest children with her. But separation remained part of life for a slave woman. Around the age of ten, a child might be taken from her. Many children were sold to another master or willed away as a gift. One fourteen-year-old black girl named Hagar kept running away from the man she'd been sold to. She always ran back to her parents. A runaway notice in the *Maryland Gazette* warned that Hagar was probably being hidden "in some Negro Quarter [cabin] as her father and mother Encourage her Elopements."

Even if African American family members had different owners, they often lived within a few miles of one another. One woman remembered only as Daphne was typical. She was born in 1736 on the Robert Tyler plantation. She lived on the plantation all her life, bearing ten children and working for six different masters. In 1787, when Daphne was about fifty years old, she still lived with four of her children and some of her grandchildren. Other grandchildren lived nearby.

THE GREAT AWAKENING

The seventeenth century had cast the Bible's Eve as temptress and troublemaker. This image was transformed during the eighteenth century. Eve became the ideal woman, "the Mother of all that Live unto God," as clergyman Cotton Mather preached. Eve's beauty, once considered sinfully seductive, became an asset. One 1727 poem even described her as "heav'nly fair, divinely beauteous Eve."

During the 1740s, a religious revival known as the Great Awakening swept the colonies. Women flocked to hear preachers such as

Jonathan Edwards. His emotional sermons left listeners sobbing and trembling on their knees. "Consider the fearful danger you are in," Edwards thundered. He described sinners hanging "by a slender thread" over the fiery pit of hell. Meanwhile "the devil," he warned, "stands ready."

Edwards may have inherited his preaching gift from his mother. Esther Stoddard Edwards held regular religious meetings in her home for female neighbors. Many women dated "their first permanent attention to religion from the impression here made," wrote a meeting regular.

Women became the backbone of eighteenth-century churches. In some churches, women made up nearly 70 percent of the congregation. For many of them, religion offered a sense of self-worth. Sermons and Bible readings stressed the importance of virtues such as humility, charity, and gentleness. Women were viewed as more devoted to religion and more spiritual than men. Yet most men considered the study of religion (theology) well beyond a woman's understanding.

African American women also found comfort in religion. Many learned Christianity from their masters or mistresses. Slaves mixed Christian beliefs with elements of African religions such as African dancing, calling responses, and prayers to ancestors. Many enslaved people identified with the Bible's stories of slavery, suffering, and eventual liberation and salvation.

TOWN LIFE

In the 1770s, nearly 90 percent of colonists lived on farms. Orchards and fields of tobacco and grains had replaced towering forests.

The smaller percentage of women who lived in towns enjoyed great advantages. They could browse streets lined with shops, looking for the latest goods from England. They could buy all kinds of prepared foods. They could hire other women to help with housework.

Towns also offered culture and up-to-date news. For entertainment, people donned their best clothes, doused their hair or wigs with white powder, and danced to stately minuets or heart-pounding jigs and reels.

They bet on horse races and attended theaters. Like good English people, colonists torched the sky with fireworks for royal English anniversaries, weddings, and birthdays. A Maryland woman described such an occasion. "An universal Mirth and Glee reigns... amongst all Ranks of People.... Musick and Dancing are the everlasting Delights."

Town life also possessed a darker side. Kitchen slop, horse manure, even rotting animal carcasses clogged city streets. The filthy conditions supplied perfect breeding grounds for epidemic disease.

Towns also sheltered a growing number of poor widows and children. Civic leaders hoped to "encourage Industry and the Employment of the Poor." The government created work for women in places like Boston's Workhouse and New York's Poor House. Pennsylvania hired out women to sew, pull flax, and work in the fields. The government also removed children from poor mothers and put the youngsters to work. In general, people viewed poverty as a mark of immorality or laziness.

A TAPESTRY OF LIVES

Women in colonial America won praise as "honored mothers," "obedient wives," and "virtuous maidens." They lived in a society defined by men and tried to live up to the expectations of that world.

Each colonial woman was an individual, yet today, most of their stories remain lost beneath centuries. But sometimes a woman steps forward.

Esther Edwards Burr was the daughter of the well-known preacher Jonathan Edwards. In April 1757, Esther wrote a friend:

> I have had a Smart Combat with Mr. Ewing.... He did not think women knew what Friendship was. They were hardly capable of anything so cool & rational as friendship—(My Tongue you know hangs pretty loose, ...) I retorted several severe things unto him before he had time to speak again.... We carried on the dispute for an hour— I talked him quite silent.

Esther died in 1758 at age twenty-six, but this trace of her independent spirit has endured. She would not rest while the honor of women's friendships was disputed—perhaps because she knew the value of those friendships firsthand. One of Esther's friends, Sarah Prince, described her grief at losing Esther. "My whole Prospects in this world are now Changed. . . ," Sarah wrote. "She laid out herself for my good. . . . O the tenderness which tied our hearts!"

The lives of Native American women, black women, and white women are woven together into the fabric of colonial life. Through their labor, their griefs, and their joys, women helped transform the New World. Many of them paid a high price for this changing world.

Anne Bradstreet summed up much of a woman's outlook on the mingled losses and blessings of colonial life. "If we had no winter, the spring would not be so pleasant," Bradstreet wrote. "If we did not sometimes taste of adversity, prosperity would not be so welcome."

A mother and her daughters tend a family garden together in the mid-1700s. The work of generations of colonial women nourished the growth of a nation.

COLONIAL WOMEN'S CLOTHING

In the 1600s and 1700s, most people owned few garments. Making a shirt, petticoat, or dress, required money, time, and effort. European investment companies even lured colonists to the New World by offering them new clothes.

A woman's clothes reflected her status in society. A dress's fabric, the richness of its trim (such as ribbon and lace), and its cleanliness pointed to the wearer's wealth or poverty. The wealthiest women could afford silk or velvet. Most women dressed in wool or linen, sometimes woven in their own households.

Seventeenth Century

This English print from 1640 shows a well-to-do, though plainly dressed, woman. She wears a man-styled beaver felt hat—a European fashion craze that kept Native American fur trappers busy. The woman's head seems separated from her body by a standing ruff. The ruff was starched or even wired into shape. Her dress features another seventeenth-century fashion favorite, a starched linen collar lying over her shoulders. Rounds of lace trim the collar, a sign of status. The puffy sleeves ending just below the elbows are also lace trimmed.

Beneath the trim peaks the sleeve of her shift, a woman's undergarment. She also wears a stiffened corset and layers of heavy petticoats. The long white apron protects her clothes.

Eighteenth Century

A women in the mid-1700s still wore a linen shift, boned-corset, and layers of petticoats beneath her dress. But the shape of her dress had changed. A well-to-do woman might add a support hoop of whalebone or cane tied around her waist. Called panniers, the side hoops held out her full gown over her hips, while the dress hung flat in front and back. Along with a cone-shaped corset, panniers gave the illusion of a small waist—a high-fashion necessity.

The eighteenth-century gown featured a low, square neckline. Modest women covered up with a lace or linen scarf crossed over the chest. Eighteenth-century sleeves were tight and elbow length. On special occasions, wealthy women might wear powdered wigs, or have their own hair piled high, oiled, and then dusted with powder or flour.

People with money ordered clothes, fabrics, and accessories directly from London merchants. Others waited for fashion dolls, dressed in the latest styles, to arrive in American shops from Europe. Fans, gloves, and handkerchiefs became favorite accessories.

SELECTED BIBLIOGRAPHY

Arber, Edward, editor. *Travels and Works of Captain John Smith, 1580–1631.* Edinburgh, Scotland: John Grant, 1910.

Axtell, James. *Beyond 1492: Encounters in Colonial North America.* New York: Oxford University Press, 1992.

———, editor. *The Indian Peoples of Eastern America: A Documentary History of the Sexes.* New York: Oxford University Press, 1981.

Berkin, Carol. *First Generations: Women in Colonial America.* New York: Hill & Wang, 1996.

Carr, Lois G., and Lorena Walsh. "The Planter's Wife: The Experience of White Women in Seventeenth-Century Maryland." *William & Mary Quarterly,* October 1977.

David, Richard, editor. *Hakluyt's Voyages: Principall Navigations, Voiages, and Discoveries of the English Nation.* Reprint, Boston, MA: Houghton Mifflin, 1981.

Demos, John. *Tried and True: Native American Women Confronting Colonization.* New York: Oxford University Press, 1995.

Dunn, Richard. "John Winthrop Writes His Journal." *William & Mary Quarterly,* April 1984.

Jones, Jacqueline. *American Work: Four Centuries of Black and White Labor.* New York: W. W. Norton, 1998.

Kamensky, Jane. *The Colonial Mosaic: American Women, 1600–1760.* New York: Oxford University Press, 1995.

Koehler, Lyle. "The Case of American Jezebels: Anne Hutchinson and Female Agitation during the Years of Antinomian Turmoil, 1636–1640." *William & Mary Quarterly,* January 1974.

Kulikoff, Allan. *Tobacco and Slaves: The Development of Southern Culture in the Chesapeake, 1680–1800.* Chapel Hill, NC: University of North Carolina Press, 1986.

Miller, John C. *The First Frontier: Life in Colonial America.* Lanham, MD: University Press of America, 1986.

Moynihan, Ruth B., et al., editors. *Second to None: A Documentary History of American Women.* Vol. 1. Lincoln, NE: University of Nebraska Press, 1993.

Pearce, Roy H., editor. *Colonial American Writing.* New York: Holt, Rinehart, and Winston, 1969.

Purvis, Thomas L. *Colonial America to 1763.* New York: Facts on File, 1999.

Rae, Noel, editor. *Witnessing America: The Library of Congress Book of Firsthand Accounts of Life in America, 1600–1900.* New York: Stonesong Press, 1996.

Ransome, David. "Wives for Virginia, 1621." *William & Mary Quarterly,* January 1991.

Spruill, Julia C. *Women's Life and Work in the Southern Colonies.* 1938. Reprint, New York: W. W. Norton, 1972.

Ulrich, Laurel. *Goodwives: Image and Reality in the Lives of Women in Northern New England, 1650–1750.* New York: Alfred A. Knopf, 1982.

Wright, Louis B. *The Cultural Life of the American Colonies.* New York: Harper and Brothers, 1957.

FURTHER READING AND WEBSITES

I believe it's always best, when possible, to let people from the past speak for themselves. I've listed several books in my Selected Bibliography that give firsthand accounts written by men and women in the 1600s and 1700s, such as *The Indian Peoples of Eastern America: A Documentary History of the Sexes* and *Second to None: A Documentary History of American Women,* Volume I. If you'd like to dig deeper into colonial history, let me suggest a few favorite books and websites.

Bradstreet, Anne. *The Complete Works of Anne Bradstreet.* Boston: Twayne Publishers, 1981. Readers can page through Bradstreet's collected poetry in this volume.

Cobblestone magazine has devoted many issues to colonial American themes. The November 2001 issue, for example, has an article called "Arts and Crafts of the Middle Atlantic Colonies."

Day, Nancy. *Your Travel Guide to Colonial America.* Minneapolis: Runestone Press, 2001.

Hakim, Joy. *The First Americans and Making Thirteen Colonies.* New York: Oxford University Press, 1993.

Miller, Brandon Marie. *Dressed for the Occasion: What Americans Wore 1620–1970.* Minneapolis: Lerner Publications Company, 1999. For more on colonial fashions and clothing, try the first few chapters.

————. *Just What the Doctor Ordered: The History of American Medicine.* Minneapolis: Lerner Publications Company, 1997. For more gruesome details of health and medicine in colonial times, take a look at the first three chapters.

Speare, Elizabeth. *The Witch of Blackbird Pond.* New York: Random House, 1959. I first read Speare's novel in sixth grade. It has remained one of my favorite books ever since. A Newbery winner for best book in children's literature, it tells the story of Kit Tyler, who tries her hardest to fit in with her Puritan relatives in 1680s Connecticut.

Wilson, Lori Lee. *The Salem Witch Trials.* Minneapolis: Lerner Publications Company, 1997. A good source for the history and hysteria surrounding the Salem Witch Trials.

<http://www.APVA.org> *The Association for the Preservation of Virginia Antiquities (APVA) and the Jamestown Rediscovery* site invites visitors to check out artifacts, archaeology of the Jamestown fort, and information about life in the first permanent English colony.

<http://www.History.org/Almanack/almanack.cfm> *The History Explorer of Colonial Williamsburg* site offers information about eighteenth-century city and colonial life.

<http://www.law.umkc.edu/faculty/projects/ftrials/salem/salem.htm> *The Salem Witchcraft Trials* site features arrest warrants, documents, biographies, paintings, and prints associated with the Salem Witch Trials.

<http://www.plimoth.org> *Plimoth-on-Web* lets users explore "The Living History Museum of Seventeenth-Century Plymouth." Check out the *Mayflower,* a Wampanoag village, and details about a colonist's life.

INDEX

ACKNOWLEDGMENTS

The photographs and illustrations in this book are used with the permission of: Library of Congress, pp. 2, [LC-USZ62-55353 and LC-USZ62-55354], 6 [LC-USZ62-56850], 8 [LC-USZ62-55353], 12 [LC-USZ62-54018], 16 [LC-USZ262-60373], 20 [LC-USZ62-873], 20 [LC-USZ62-55353], 22 [LC-USZ62-1495], 30 [LC-USZ62-55353], 36 [LC-USZ62-3291], 40 [LC-USZ62-55353], 43 [LC-USZ62-78099], 51 [LC-USZ62-29058], 52 [LC-USZ62-55353], 58 [PS-712-C25RBD Rare book division], 62 [LC-USZ62-55353], 67 [LC-USZ62-97560], 73 [LC-USZ62-476], 74 [LC-USZ62-20966], 76 [LC-USZC4-723], 79 [LC-USZ62-1473], 88; © Bettmann/ CORBIS, pp. 8, 29, 32, 56, 89; Laura Westlund, pp. 10, 41; North Wind Pictures, pp. 13, 15, 38, 45, 48, 52, 57, 62, 66, 82; James Ford Bell Library, University of Minnesota, p. 14; Colonial Williamsburg Foundation [1997-86-CN], p. 19; Library of Virginia [Neg. A9-10097], p. 23; © Hulton|Archive/Getty Images, pp. 26, 28, 30, 35; The Granger Collection, p. 31; © 2002 Museum of Fine Arts, Boston, p. 40; Maryland Historical Society, Baltimore, Maryland, p. 49; Philadelphia Museum of Art: Gift of the Barra Foundation, Inc., p. 55; The Schlessinger Library, Radcliffe Institute, Harvard University, p. 61; Worchester Art Museum, Worchester, Massachusetts: Gift of Mr. and Mrs. Albert W. Rice, p. 69; © CORBIS, p. 77; From the collections of Henry Ford Museum and Greefield Village (Neg. No. B45456, Acc. No. 30.471.27), p. 80; Connecticut Historical Society, p. 83 [1962.28.4]; Courtesy of the Wethersfield Historical Society, p. 87.

Cover and chapter icons courtesy of the Library of Congress [LC-USZ62-55353 and LC-USZ62-55354].

TITLES FROM THE AWARD-WINNING PEOPLE'S HISTORY SERIES:

For more information, please call 1-800-328-4929 or visit www.lernerbooks.com